# NELSON KEY GEOG
# Connections
## Teacher's Handbook

**5th Edition**

THE CEDARS SCHOOL
Coombe Road
Croydon, CR0 5RD
Tel: 020 8185 7770

**CATHERINE HURST AND GUY MORTIMER**

**DAVID WAUGH AND TONY BUSHELL**

OXFORD
UNIVERSITY PRESS

Great Clarendon Street, Oxford, OX2 6DP, United Kingdom

Oxford University Press is a department of the University of Oxford. It furthers the University's objective of excellence in research, scholarship, and education by publishing worldwide. Oxford is a registered trade mark of Oxford University Press in the UK and in certain other countries

© Oxford University Press 2014

Authors: Catherine Hurst and Guy Mortimer

The moral rights of the authors have been asserted

First published in 2012

This edition 2014

All rights reserved. No part of this publication may be reproduced, stored in a retrieval system, or transmitted, in any form or by any means, without the prior permission in writing of Oxford University Press, or as expressly permitted by law, by licence or under terms agreed with the appropriate reprographics rights organization. Enquiries concerning reproduction outside the scope of the above should be sent to the Rights Department, Oxford University Press, at the address above.

You must not circulate this work in any other form and you must impose this same condition on any acquirer

British Library Cataloguing in Publication Data
Data available

978-1-40 852733-7

10 9 8 7 6 5 4 3 2 1

Paper used in the production of this book is a natural, recyclable product made from wood grown in sustainable forests.
The manufacturing process conforms to the environmental regulations of the country of origin.

Printed in Spain by Graphycems

**Acknowledgements**

The publishers would like to thank the following for permission to use photographs and other copyright material:

Illustrations by Kathy Baxendale, Nick Hawken, Angela Knowles, Gordon Lawson, GreenGate Publishing Services, Richard Morris, David Russell, Tim Smith, John Yorke

Cover photographs: FTFoxfoto/Fotalia; Vision/Fotalia; Rainer Albeiz//Shutterstock; TA Crafts/iStockphoto

Every effort has been made to contact copyright holders of material reproduced in this book. Any omissions will be rectified in subsequent printings if notice is given to the publisher.

Links to third party websites are provided by Oxford in good faith and for information only. Oxford disclaims any responsibility for the materials contained in any third party website referenced in this work.

# Contents

| How to use this book | 5 |
|---|---|

## 1 Rivers, coasts and glaciation

| | |
|---|---|
| What is weathering? | 6 |
| What is erosion … and how can it help shape the land? | 7 |
| How do rivers shape the land? | 8 |
| What causes waterfalls? | 9 |
| What happens on a river bend? | 10 |
| How does the sea shape the coast? | 11 |
| What is the coastal erosion problem? | 12 |
| How can coastal erosion be reduced? | 13 |
| How does ice shape the land? | 14 |
| What landforms result from glaciation? | 15 |

## 2 Economic activity

| | |
|---|---|
| What types of economic activity are there? | 16 |
| What are the main types of farming in Britain? | 17 |
| What is a hill sheep farm like?/What is an arable farm like? | 18 |
| What is the best site for a factory?/Choosing the right site – the iron and steel industry | 19 |
| Choosing the right site – the car industry | 20 |
| What is the tourist industry? | 21 |
| Where do the tourists go? | 22 |
| What are high-tech industries? | 23 |
| Where are high-tech industries located? | 24 |
| The economic activity enquiry | 25 |

## 3 Population

| | |
|---|---|
| Are we spread evenly? | 26 |
| What affects where we live? | 27 |
| Where do we live? | 28 |
| How does population change? | 29 |
| What is migration? | 30 |
| Who migrates to the UK? | 31 |
| What are the effects of migration? | 32 |
| How can we compare local areas? | 33 |
| The population enquiry | 34 |

## 4 India and Asia

| | |
|---|---|
| What are Asia's main physical features? | 35 |
| What are Asia's main human features? | 36 |
| India – a land of contrasts | 37 |
| What are India's main physical features? | 38 |
| What are India's main population features? | 39 |
| What's it like living in Mumbai? | 40 |
| What's it like living in a village in India? | 41 |
| How interdependent is India? | 42 |
| The India enquiry? | 43 |

## 5 World issues

| | |
|---|---|
| What is climate change? | 44 |
| What are the effects of climate change? | 45 |
| How can our energy use change? | 46 |
| What is the water problem? | 47 |
| Food – too little or too much? | 48 |
| What is the poverty problem? | 49 |
| How might poverty be reduced? | 50 |
| The world issues enquiry | 51 |

## 6 Key skills: maps and diagrams

| | |
|---|---|
| How can we use an atlas? | 52 |
| How can we describe physical features on a map? | 53 |
| How can we describe human features on a map? | 54 |
| What do choropleth maps show? | 55 |
| How can we use diagrams in geography? | 56 |
| What are population pyramids? | 57 |

## Appendices

| | |
|---|---|
| Appendix 1: The economic activity enquiry checklist | 58 |
| Appendix 2: The population enquiry checklist | 59 |
| Appendix 3: The India enquiry checklist | 60 |
| Appendix 4: The resources enquiry checklist | 61 |

# How to use this book

This Teacher's Handbook has been written to accompany the *Nelson Key Geography Connections* pupil book. It is intended to provide:

- full support for newly qualified teachers
- ideas for experienced, but busy, geography teachers
- ideas for experienced teachers who are not geographers.

Its aim is to provide succinct, at-a-glance information specifically to:

- help provide teachers plan and deliver high-quality geography lessons
- provide support, ideas, and suggestions for the use of additional resources
- explain the geographical content of each unit
- provide answers to the activities in the pupil book.

Where items are included here as suggestions, i.e. the Skills builders and Differentiation suggestions, they are intended to be just that. They are not meant to be prescriptive. You may want to use them as they stand, or they may spark off other, better, ideas that you can use.

# 1 Rivers, coasts and glaciation

**Pupil Book pages 6–7**

# What is weathering?

## About this spread

This spread looks at weathering. It examines how frost action, temperature change, chemical and biological processes can attack and rot away the landscape. The aim is to show the great variety of scenery that there is in the world, as well as how there is always some type of weathering going on – whatever the location, climate, rock type or vegetation cover.

## Learning outcomes

By the end of this spread pupils should be able to:

- define the term 'weathering'
- list four types of weathering
- describe how different types of weathering work.

## Key vocabulary

- landscape
- weathering
- erosion
- freeze–thaw weathering
- onion-skin weathering
- biological weathering
- chemical weathering

## Learning objectives

On this spread pupils should learn:

- that the surface of the earth and the landscapes around us are constantly changing
- that the changes are a result of weathering and erosion
- that weathering occurs when rocks are attacked by the weather, plants and animals.

## Skills builder

Pupils need to develop a wide range of geographical skills and these include the ability to draw and label diagrams. Their diagrams do not need to be works of art, but they should be clear and straightforward. In Activity 3, pupils are asked to show, with the help of a diagram, how freeze–thaw weathering can break up rocks. In this instance, pupils can copy the diagram on page 6 (in the textbox on freeze–thaw weathering). They will find that there will be many instances where a well-labelled diagram provides a much better answer than text alone.

## Further discussion suggestions

- Why is freeze–thaw weathering more common in upland areas of Britain than in polar regions?
- How can chemical weathering in areas of carboniferous limestone lead to the formation of caves, stalactites and stalagmites?

## Answers to activities

**1 a and b**

Weathering is the breakdown of rocks by climate, chemicals, plants and animals.

- Sun (heat)
- Pollution (acid in rainwater)
- Rain (moisture)
- Ice/snow (cool, cold temperatures)

**2 a** Freeze–thaw weathering is what happens when water continually freezes and thaws in cracks in rocks, causing the rock to weaken and break up.

  **b** Onion-skin weathering is what happens when the outer layers of rock are continually heated and cooled, causing pieces of rock to peel off like the skin of an onion.

  **c** Chemical weathering is when acid in rainwater attacks the rock causing it to rot and crumble away.

**3** Pupils' diagrams and labelling should be similar to the diagram for freeze–thaw weathering on page 6 of the pupil book.

**4 a and b**

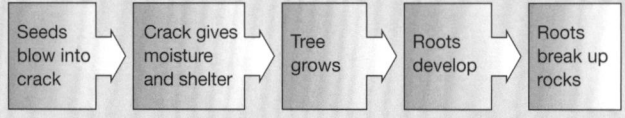

Seeds blow into crack → Crack gives moisture and shelter → Tree grows → Roots develop → Roots break up rocks

**5 a** Pupils' diagrams should be similar to the diagram in the book.

  **b** **Mount Everest, Nepal** Freeze–thaw weathering as the temperature is around 0 °C and will allow water to freeze (usually at night) and thaw during the day.

  **Monument Valley, USA** Onion skin weathering as the area is very dry and the rock is bare, so it will heat up quickly during the day, but cool at night.

  **Guilin, China** Chemical weathering as the climate is warm and wet which allows chemical reactions to occur faster.

# 1 Rivers, coasts and glaciation

**Pupil Book pages 8–9**

## What is erosion ... and how can it help shape the land?

### About this spread

This spread looks mainly at erosion. Erosion is different from weathering in that erosion always includes the removal of material. The four types of erosion described should be understood by most pupils. An understanding of erosion, transportation and deposition is important as it underpins the landform processes that follow on the next few pages. The analogy of digging in the garden (erosion), moving the material in a wheelbarrow (transportation) and then dumping it elsewhere (deposition) is one that pupils should understand. This can be linked with the idea of energy. The more energy you have, the more soil you can dig or transport.

### Learning objectives

On this spread pupils should learn:

- that weathering breaks up rocks and erosion wears away and removes the loosened material
- how different forces – rivers, ice, the sea and wind – erode the land.

### Skills builder

Throughout their study of geography, pupils need to learn about, and be able to describe and explain, a range of different processes. They will have already encountered some, such as the processes that lead to rainfall, in *Nelson Key Geography Foundations*. In this unit, pupils learn about the processes of weathering, erosion, transportation and deposition, and how these processes shape the landscape. They will then go on to learn about the different landforms created by these processes.

### Further discussion suggestions

- Glaciers erode by abrasion and by plucking. How do these work?
- How did wind erosion create the dust bowl in Oklahoma and Texas in the 1930s?

### Learning outcomes

By the end of this spread pupils should be able to:

- define the term 'erosion'
- describe the difference between erosion and weathering
- describe how erosion, transportation and deposition help to shape the land.

### Key vocabulary

- glacier
- waves
- current
- load
- erosion
- transportation
- deposition

### Answers to activities

1. **a** Items should be listed in the following order (hardest first): diamond, steel, plastic, wood, rubber, chalk, soap.

   **b** The two that would be most difficult to wear down are the hardest two, i.e. diamond and steel.

   **c** Pupils can choose any three items and need to suggest how they might be worn down. Responses will vary.

2. The three correct statements are as follows:
   - Weathering is the breakdown of rock by nature.
   - Erosion is the wearing away of rock.
   - Erosion includes the removal of loose material.

3. **a**, **b** and **c**

| Type | Description |
|---|---|
| Banks eroded — River | **Erosion by rivers** Rivers wear away rock from the bed, and erode the banks on either side of the channel. When a river is in flood, large boulders might be loosened and rolled down the river bed. |
| Force of waves — Sea erodes coast | **Erosion by the sea** The action of waves constantly hitting rocks causes the rock to weaken and pieces to break off. |
| Glacier — Side and floor of valley eroded | **Erosion by ice** Stones and boulders that fall onto a glacier freeze into the ice and act like sandpaper, wearing away the rocks on the valley sides and bottom. |
| Rocks eroded into strange shapes — Wind | **Erosion by the wind** The wind picks up tiny particles of sand and blasts them against rock, eroding it. |

4. The pupil may come up with other ideas, but for those mentioned:

   - Bulldozer:
     erosion, digging a hole
     transportation, moving it to the side of the hole
     deposition, placing it in a pile.
   - Washing dishes:
     erosion, using a cloth to remove stuck-on food
     transportation, food floating in the sink
     deposition, food getting stuck in the plughole.
   - Sandpapering wood:
     erosion, rubbing the wood and creating wood-dust
     transportation, sweeping up the wood-dust
     deposition, placing it in the bin.

# 1 Rivers, coasts and glaciation

## Pupil Book pages 10–11
## How do rivers shape the land?

### About this spread

This spread investigates how rivers shape the land and looks at some of the landforms found in a river's upper course. Erosion, weathering, transportation and deposition processes are all involved as rivers shape the landscape. Labelled diagrams, a photo and fieldsketch are used to help pupils understand the processes involved.

### Learning objectives

On this spread pupils should learn:

- that a river erodes downwards in its upper course
- that a river erodes because of the load it is carrying
- that a river has distinctive features in its upper course.

### Learning outcomes

By the end of this spread pupils should be able to:

- understand that rivers erode, transport and deposit material
- draw a diagram to show how a V-shaped valley is formed
- draw a sketch to show the features of a river valley in its upper course.

### Skills builder

In Activity 3, pupils are asked to copy a sketch of a photo of a V-shaped valley and add labels to it. The ability to draw sketches from photos and in the field is a skill that pupils need to develop. If they are drawing a sketch from a photo, they should start by drawing a frame for the sketch to the same dimensions as the photo. They should identify the main features they want to show and draw these in. They should then add smaller details. They need to keep the sketch clear and simple; they do not need to add everything that is in the photo. They should add labels to identify the main features, and can add further labels for description and explanation.

### Further discussion suggestions

- Water flowing downhill follows the easiest route. How does this lead to the formation of interlocking spurs?
- What are rapids? How do they form on a river?

### Answers to activities

1 Pupils' descriptions should be similar to this:

The water in a river pushes boulders, stones and rock particles along the river's course. As it does so, the loose material scrapes the river bed and banks and loosens other material. The river moves (transports) this material and drops (deposits) it somewhere else.

2 **a, b and c**

*How a V-shaped valley is formed*

As the river erodes downwards, the steep sides are attacked by weathering. This breaks up and loosens the soil and rock.

The river erodes downwards as boulders, stones and rock particles are bounced and scraped along the river bed.

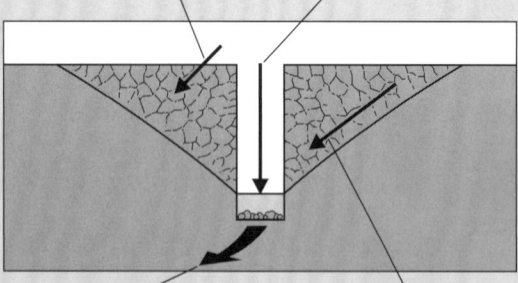

The river carries material away. The result is a steep-sided valley which is V-shaped.

The loosened material slowly moves down the slope because of gravity, or is washed into the river by rainwater.

3 **a and b**

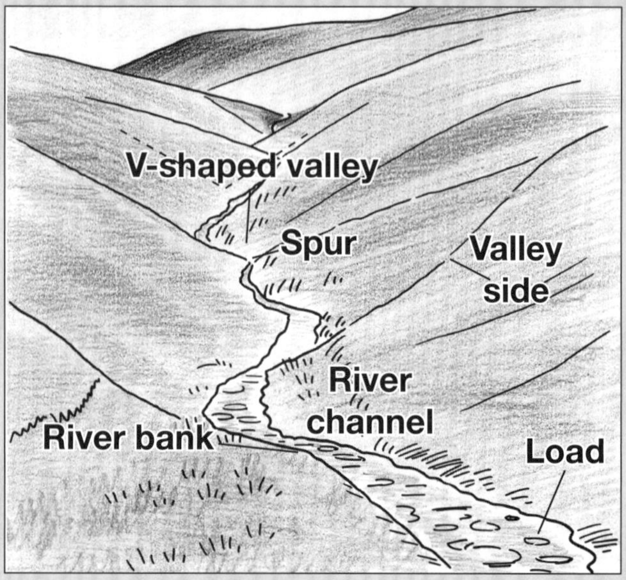

# 1 Rivers, coasts and glaciation

**Pupil Book pages 12–13**

# What causes waterfalls?

## About this spread

This spread looks at one of the more spectacular river features – waterfalls. Although waterfalls in the UK are by no means the highest in the world, they can be impressive features when a river is in flood. This spread focuses on Niagara Falls with an explanation of how the waterfall has formed. A diagram shows how the waterfall has retreated upstream. The text explains that many waterfalls are formed in the same way as Niagara Falls.

## Learning outcomes

By the end of this spread pupils should be able to:
- describe how waterfalls form
- describe how a gorge develops.

## Key vocabulary

- waterfall
- plunge pool
- gorge

## Learning objectives

On this spread pupils should learn:
- that waterfalls form when rivers flow over different types of rock.

## Skills builder

There is a lot of subject-specific terminology and key vocabulary for pupils to get to grips with in geography and this is especially so in this topic. Pupils will always achieve more highly if they use the correct terminology. One of the suggestions for a plenary activity throughout this unit is that pupils could build up their own dictionary of key vocabulary. They can use the glossary at the end of the pupil book to help them to do this. You could also help pupils to learn the meanings of terminology and key words by displaying them around the classroom, along with their definitions.

## Further discussion suggestions

- Why does a hanging valley end in a waterfall?
- Why is Bridal Veil waterfall in Yosemite National Park, USA, so named?

## Answers to activities

**1** a, b, c, d and e

Pupils' maps should look similar to this:

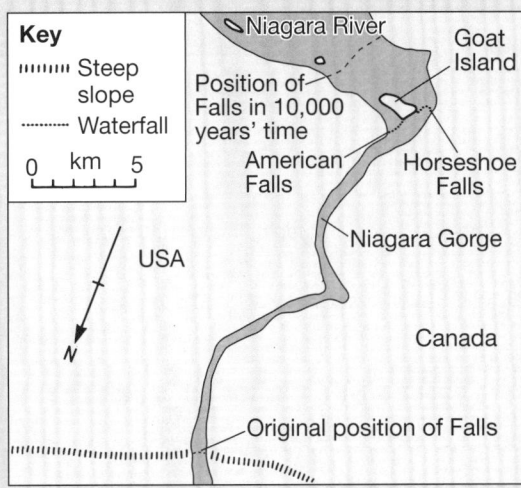

**2** a and b

Pupils' diagrams should look like this.

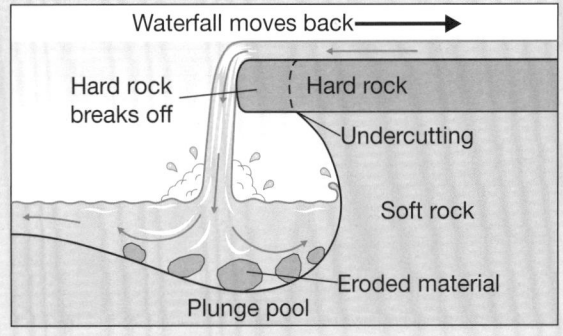

**3** Soft rock worn away → Plunge pool deepened → Hard rock undercut → Hard rock collapses → Waterfall moves back

# 1 Rivers, coasts and glaciation

**Pupil Book pages 14–15**

# What happens on a river bend?

## About this spread

Rivers rarely flow in straight lines. In their middle course they meander across the flood plain. This spread looks at how erosion occurs on the outside of the meander (or river bend), while deposition happens on the inside of the meander.

## Learning objectives

On this spread pupils should learn:

- how the processes of erosion and deposition operate on river bends
- about meanders and the flood plain.

## Learning outcomes

By the end of this spread pupils should be able to:

- understand that a river's course usually has many bends, which causes it to meander across the flood plain
- draw sketches to show deposition and erosion on river bends
- explain how the outside of a river bend is worn away by erosion, while the inside is built up by deposition.

## Key vocabulary

- current
- cross-section
- meander
- flood plain
- alluvium

## Skills builder

Using and interpreting photos is a key geographical skill. This spread provides pupils with opportunities to use ground shots and an aerial photo of meanders and a flood plain. Photos are useful because they can show what features or places are like. They can provide information and help us to understand the processes that made places and things the way they are. Ground photos show the landscape as we see it from the earth's surface. Aerial photos are taken from aircraft and can be vertical or oblique. Vertical photos are taken directly overhead, while oblique photos are taken at an angle. They can show detail of a small area or to provide a more general picture of a larger area.

See Chapter 7 of *Nelson Key Geography Foundations* for more information on using photographs in geography.

## Further discussion suggestions

- What is an ox-bow lake?
- How does an ox-bow lake form?
- Why do people risk living on flood plains?

## Answers to activities

**1 a, b and c**

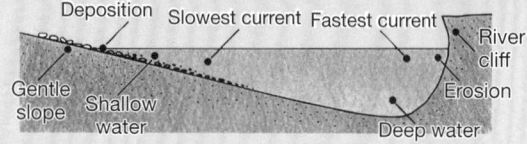

Labels: Deposition, Slowest current, Fastest current, River cliff, Gentle slope, Shallow water, Erosion, Deep water

**d** Water flows faster on the outside of the bend. Erosion takes place here and as the river bank is worn away a steep river cliff develops. The river flows more slowly on the inside of the bend, so deposition takes place and material builds up there.

**2 a**

Deposition on the inside of a river bend

Erosion on the outside of a river bend

**b** The sketch of photo B shows a small beach on the inside of a river bend. The sketch of photo C shows a river cliff on the outside of a river bend.

**c** Water is flowing slowly on the inside of the bend. Material builds up here owing to deposition forming a beach, which makes the bank gently sloping. The fastest current is on the outside of the bend. Where water hits the bank it causes erosion, which deepens the river channel and wears away the bank to create a river cliff.

**3** Meander is the name for a bend in a river.

The flood plain is an area of flat land on either side of the river channel. When a river overflows its banks this area is covered in water.

Alluvium is the fine muddy material that is left behind after flooding. It is also called silt.

**4** Student responses will vary. Answers could include:

- It is easy to use machinery such as a combine harvester on flat land.
- Flood plains get covered in nutrient rich silt which increases crop yield.
- There is a good water source that can be used as a source of irrigation.

**5** Student responses will vary. Answers could include:

- Flooding can destroy crops.
- Flooding can cause distress to animals. They could even die.
- Land can be very marshy and crops won't grow well in the wet conditions.
- It is easy for fertiliser to run into the river and pollute it.

The problem can be reduced by:

- Building flood banks will allow the channel to carry more water and would be less likely to flood.
- Dams will trap water upstream and it can be released slowly when there is less chance of a flood.
- Dredging will make the channel deeper so it can carry more water and reduce the chances of flooding – although this can have a negative environmental affect.

# 1 Rivers, coasts and glaciation

**Pupil Book pages 16–17**

# How does the sea shape the coast?

## About this spread

This spread looks at how the processes of erosion, transportation and deposition operate on the coast to produce some amazing coastal landforms. Landforms created by erosion include caves, arches and stacks, headlands and bays. Those created by deposition include beaches and spits. These are all covered on this spread.

## Learning objectives

On this spread pupils should learn:

- that the sea erodes, transports and deposits material to produce different coastal landforms
- about some of the erosion and deposition landforms found on the coast.

## Learning outcomes

By the end of this spread pupils should be able to:

- understand that the coastline is always changing as a result of the processes of erosion and deposition
- explain how caves, arches and stacks form
- describe the formation of a spit.

## Skills builder

This spread reinforces the importance of the processes of erosion, transportation and deposition as major land-forming agents. Earlier in this unit, pupils studied these processes in connection with rivers. They are key geographical processes that pupils need to understand, so it does no harm to revisit them in a different context here.

## Further discussion suggestions

- What is longshore drift, and how does it create spits?
- How does a stack become a stump?
- How can coastal deposition form a lagoon?

## Key vocabulary

- erosion landform
- bay
- headland
- arch
- stack
- beach
- deposition landform
- spit

## Answers to activities

**1 a, b and d**

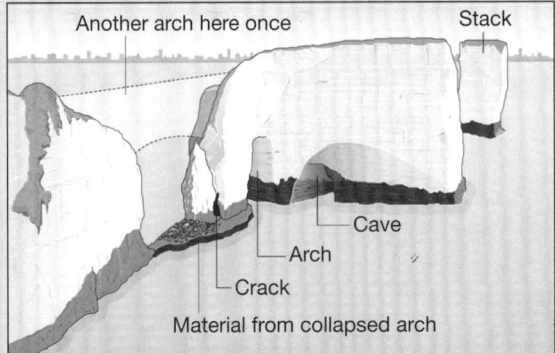

c  Arches form as a result of coastal erosion. The sea attacks small cracks in cliffs by bombarding them with pieces of loose rock. Continued erosion means the cracks get larger and develop into caves. If a cave is eroded through a headland, an arch forms.

**2 a and b**

Pupils should label the drawings of Spurn Head spit (as below) and also write an explanation similar to the following on the formation of the spit. Erosion occurs on the coastline around Flamborough Head, north of Spurn Head. Transportation by sea currents moves the eroded material down the coast. Deposition occurs where the coastline changes direction. The spit grows out from the coast as more material builds up. The end of the spit is curved by the action of the waves. The spit is 6 km long.

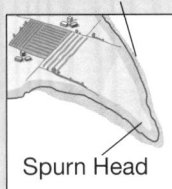

Eroded material transported down the coast

Spurn Head

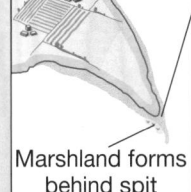

Material dropped where coast changes direction and spit grows out from coast

Marshland forms behind spit

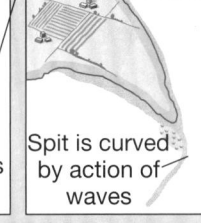

Spit is curved by action of waves

## 1 Rivers, coasts and glaciation

**Pupil Book pages 18–19**

# What is the coastal erosion problem?

## About this spread

This spread looks at the problem of coastal erosion. The east coast of England has some of the fastest-eroding coastlines in Europe and at Holderness in Yorkshire the coast is retreating by about 2 metres a year. This spread considers why erosion is worse along the Holderness coast than on other parts of the coastline and considers some of the problems erosion causes.

## Learning objectives

On this spread pupils should learn:

- that coastal erosion is a problem for parts of the British Isles
- why erosion is a major problem along the Holderness coast.

## Learning outcomes

By the end of this spread pupils should be able to:

- understand that the east coast of England has some of the fastest eroding coastlines in Europe
- describe the processes at work on the Holderness coast
- list the problems caused by erosion in the Holderness area.

## Skills builder

Pupils will use maps throughout their study of geography. The maps included in the *Nelson Key Geography* pupil books are not decorative. They convey key geographical information, and pupils need to be able to interpret them. The captions tell them what the map is about, and the text and activities will help them to understand and read the maps. On this spread pupils not only have to extract information from the maps, but they also have to use the scale lines to measure distance. Pages 94 and 95 of *Nelson Key Geography Foundations* illustrate how to measure distance on a map. There is also an animation showing how to use this skill available on Kerboodle.

## Further discussion suggestions

- Why is removing offshore shingle for construction purposes a bad idea?
- How do sandbanks form? Why are they a danger to shipping?
- What is a wave-cut platform?

## Answers to activities

1  **a**  The coastline has moved back up to 5 km in 2,000 years.

   **b**  26 villages have been lost.

   **c**  The winds come from the north-east and drive the waves against the coast. Grimsby is protected from the winds and waves by Spurn Head, and so the coast there has not been affected by erosion.

2  **a**  The coastline has moved back approximately 125 m in 30 years.

   **b**  Ten buildings have been lost.

   **c**  The post office and the school should soon be closed down.

3  **Buildings**

- Houses have fallen into the sea.
- Farm buildings have become unsafe.
- Post office in Mappleton is under threat.
- The school in Mappleton is under threat.

**Industries**

- Farming is affected, as much farmland has been lost.
- Tourism may be affected, as seaside resorts such as Hornsea and Withernsea are under threat.
- Two gas plants on the coast are at risk.

**Employment**

- Farmland and farms have been lost, so farming jobs are likely to have been lost too.
- Jobs may be lost in tourism if the seaside resorts are affected.
- Jobs may be lost if the gas plants are forced to close.

4  Pupils' reasons for and against living in Mappleton may vary, but could include the following.

**For** it is on the coast; it is near to Hornsea where many people work; it is also near to the gas plant – another source of employment.

**Against** houses have already fallen into the sea; farm buildings have become unsafe; part of the coastal road has been lost to the sea; industries and jobs may be lost.

# 1 Rivers, coasts and glaciation

**Pupil Book pages 20–21**

# How can coastal erosion be reduced?

## About this spread

This spread continues the work on pages 18–19 and looks at how the problem of coastal erosion can be managed. It considers some of the different methods used to help reduce coastal erosion and what can be done to protect the Holderness coast. Three possible options for the Holderness coast are considered: building sea defences along the entire coastline, protecting just the main towns, or doing nothing at all.

## Learning outcomes

By the end of this spread pupils should be able to:

- give the arguments for and against protecting the coastline from erosion
- assess the advantages and disadvantages of alternative methods of coastal defences.

## Key vocabulary

- sea walls
- beach rebuilding
- groynes
- rip-rap

## Learning objectives

On this spread pupils should learn:

- about the ways in which coastal erosion can be reduced
- that protecting one part of the coast can cause worse problems further along the coast.

## Skills builder

Activity 1b of the pupil book provides an opportunity for pupils to use their maths skills in a geographical context. Pupils have to work out the cost of protecting 60 km of coastline using different methods. In other topics in geography, pupils will have opportunities to use their maths skills in a number of ways including:

- drawing graphs
- interpreting graphs
- working out and using percentages and ratios
- investigating growth rates.

## Further discussion suggestions

- What is the difference between hard and soft engineering in terms of coastal defences?
- Could wave energy be reduced or diverted by building offshore breakwaters?

## Answers to activities

1. a
   - Rip-rap would be easiest to build, as boulders and concrete blocks are simply piled up.
   - Beach rebuilding would be the most attractive to look at.
   - Beach rebuilding would cause the fewest problems for people using the beach.

   b The cost of protecting 60 km of the Holderness coast for each method would be:

   sea walls = £420 million; beach rebuilding = £120 million; groynes = £450 million; rip-rap = £180 million.

2. The arguments against protecting the whole coastline include:
   - cost
   - most of the coastline consists of farmland (low value and possibly not worth protecting)
   - not protecting the whole coast helps retain wildlife and the quality of the natural environment
   - protecting the whole coast may create more problems elsewhere, e.g. Spurn Head might disappear.

3. a Pupils might choose any of the three solutions listed on page 21 of the pupil book.

   b Pupils' descriptions should match those on page 21 of the pupil book.

   c The advantages and disadvantages of the schemes are largely given on page 21 of the pupil book. Pupils might include additional information from page 20.

# 1 Rivers, coasts and glaciation

**Pupil Book pages 22–23**

# How does ice shape the land?

## About this spread

This spreads examines how glacial process can affect upland areas through the processes of erosion, deposition and transportation. It explains how plucking, abrasion and freeze–thaw weathering create pieces of rock, how these pieces are transported by the glacier and where they might be deposited. It also looks at the landforms that are left behind after these processes have occurred and the characteristic features of corries, arêtes and pyramidal peaks.

## Learning objectives

On this spread pupils should learn:

- the types of erosion, transportation and deposition associated with a glacier
- to describe the landforms found in upland glacier areas.

## Learning outcomes

By the end of this spread pupils should be able to:

- identify where different processes occur in a glacial landscape
- annotate examples of glacial landscapes in the Alps.

## Skills builder

Pupils often use diagrams and photos and it is an important skill to be able to interpret what is happening in both an idealised version of a situation and a similar real world example. Photos are useful because they can show what features or places are like, they can provide information, and help us to understand the processes that made places and things the way they are. Pupils have the opportunity to build their skills by linking key words, diagrams and photographs.

## Key vocabulary

- glaciers
- erosion
- transportation
- deposition
- moraine
- freeze–thaw weathering
- plucking
- abrasion
- corrie
- arête
- pyramidal peak

## Further discussion suggestions

- Which areas of the world will we find these landforms in?
- When will freeze–thaw weathering be most effective?
- What is the role of gravity in the process?

## Answers to activities

**1 a** A glacier is a slow moving river of ice.

**b** The force of gravity causes a glacier to move downhill.

**c** Moraine are the rocks and sediment carried and deposited by a glacier.

**2 a and b**

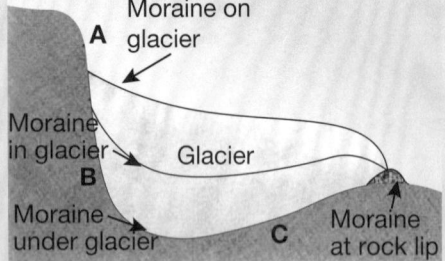

**c** **A** Freeze–thaw: water sits in cracks in the rock, freezes, expands and puts pressure on the rock. The ice thaws, the crack refills with water and the whole process starts again. Eventually pieces of rock break off.

**B** Plucking: ice freezes to the rock and pulls it away when the glacier moves.

**C** Abrasion: rocks at the base of the glacier sandpaper the bottom of the corrie.

**3 a** Pupils make their own sketch of Photo D.

**b**

**c** Glaciers form on the side of the Matterhorn when ice does not melt.

Freeze–thaw, plucking and abrasion create a number of armchair-shaped hollows called corries.

A knife-shaped ridge, called an arête, forms where two corries form back-to-back.

When several arêtes meet, a pyramidal peak forms, like that seen on the Matterhorn.

# 1 Rivers, coasts and glaciation

**Pupil Book pages 24–25**

## What landforms result from glaciation?

### About this spread

This spread continues the work on pages 22–23 and looks at how a glacier influences a more lowland landscape. It considers what the landscape may look like as a river valley before glaciation, when it is ice filled and when the ice has melted. By looking at these three time periods it allows the pupils to consider how landforms created by the river will be altered by a glacier. It also introduces pupils to landforms such as hanging valleys, ribbon lakes and truncated spurs.

### Learning objectives

On this spread pupils should learn:

- about the landforms created in the lower part of a glacier.
- to compare the landforms formed by a glacier and a river.

### Skills builder

The pupils have the opportunity to practise drawing sketches of landforms and to identify and label the key features. This is an important skill as it allows pupils to interpret the landscape that they are looking at. To help increase the level of complexity contained within the sketch, pupils could add annotations with connectives such as 'because', 'this means' or 'so that'. The activities also provide an opportunity for pupils to practise the skill of explaining a process ensuring that they use the correct geographical terminology and the correct order in which processes occur.

### Learning outcomes

By the end of this spread pupils should be able to:

- identify glacial landforms
- explain how a glacier forms a glacial trough
- explain how river landforms are changed by glaciers.

### Key vocabulary

- V-shaped valley
- U-shaped valley
- glacial trough
- truncated spur
- hanging valley
- ribbon lake
- erratic

### Further discussion suggestions

- Which areas of the world would we find these landscapes in?
- Are there any examples of these features close to the school? Look at the reasons why there are or are not.
- What would these features look like on an Ordnance Survey map?

### Answers to activities

1. A glacial trough is a flat-bottomed valley with steep sides that provides this feature's other name 'U-shaped valley'. A U-shaped valley forms when ice erodes a V-shaped river valley, making it deeper, wider and straighter. In a glacial trough there are no interlocking spurs as they are eroded away.

2. 
   1. pyramidal peaks
   2. hanging valley
   3. arêtes
   4. erratics
   5. corries
   6. truncated spurs
   7. ribbon lake
   8. glacial trough

3. 
   a. A U-shaped valley forms when the glacier erodes a V-shaped valley, making it deeper, wider and straighter. Fragments of rock carried along the sides of the glacier cause abrasion, removing interlocking spurs and widening and straightening the valley. The weight of the ice causes abrasion along the base of the glacier which deepens the valley.

   b. Interlocking spurs turn into truncated spurs when fragments of stone carried by the glacier erode the sides of the U-shaped valley and remove the point of the spur.

   c. Glaciers in river tributaries contain less ice so they do not erode as deeply as the ice in the glacial trough. This feature is called a hanging valley. Where the two valleys meet (a confluence) there is now a steep wall. To get to the bottom of the glacial trough from the hanging valley, the water needs to pass over the steep wall as a waterfall.

## 2 Economic activity

**Pupil Book pages 28–29**

# What types of economic activity are there?

### About this spread

This spread introduces pupils to four different sectors of the economy and provides examples of each. It looks at how the proportion of people working in each type of industry has changed from a reliance on mainly primary industry in 1810, mainly secondary in 1910, through to mainly tertiary industry in 2010. It also asks pupils to conduct a survey and gives teachers an opportunity to discuss the issues surrounding the completion of a valid survey.

### Learning outcomes

By the end of this spread pupils should be able to:

- define different types of industry
- categorise different jobs into type of industry
- conduct a survey to determine the employment structure of members of the class.

### Key vocabulary

- industry
- economic activity
- primary industries
- secondary industries
- tertiary industries
- quaternary industries
- natural resources
- manufacturing
- service industry
- employment structure

### Learning objectives

On this spread pupils should learn:

- the categories of industry that jobs can be divided into
- how employment structure has changed over time.

### Skills builder

The spread allows pupils to conduct a survey and gives them an opportunity to address various issues when conducting the survey. Some issues to consider could include, how the pupils can make their survey a fair test or what a suitable results grid may look like. The spread also allows pupils to practise their numeracy skills ensuring pupils select appropriate axes, label their axes and provide a title for the graph. If pupils decide to draw a pie chart they can be reminded that multiplying the percentage by 3.6 is a short cut for calculating angles.

### Further discussion suggestions

- How valid are any results that are collected?
- What could we do to make the results we have collected more valid?
- Which types of graph show the results in the clearest fashion?
- What is quinary industry?

### Answers to activities

1 The correct sentences are:

- Primary activities collect natural resources from land or sea.
- Secondary activities make things from natural resources.
- Tertiary activities provide a service for people.
- Quaternary activities are mainly concerned with information.

2 Primary: coal miner, forestry worker, fisherman, quarry worker, farmer.

Secondary: shoemaker, carpenter, baker, builder, sewing machinist.

Tertiary: TV presenter, nurse footballer, fire fighter, bus driver, police officer, shop assistant, pop singer.

3 **a, b** and **c**

Work in groups of at least ten so that you have enough answers to make it representative.

**d** When describing a graph you could include:

- What was the largest bar/slice in your graph? What percentage did it represent?
- What was the smallest bar/slice in your graph? What percentage did it represent?
- What was the relationship between the largest and smallest bar/slice (twice as big, three times as big).

## 2 Economic activity

**Pupil Book pages 30–31**

# What are the main types of farming in Britain?

### About this spread

In this spread pupils are asked to consider the different types of farming that they might encounter in the United Kingdom. Pupils might be familiar with arable and pastoral but this might be the first time that they have been introduced to the key words. The spread also mentions crofting as a type of farming. The pupils are asked to consider where each type of farming is based and the human and physical requirements for each type, such as relief, soil fertility or machinery.

### Learning objectives

On this spread pupils should learn:

- how to define the different types of farming that are found in the United Kingdom
- how to describe the geographic distribution of different farming types in the United Kingdom
- to give reasons for the distribution using human and physical factors.

### Learning outcomes

By the end of this spread pupils should be able to:

- define key words
- describe the different types of farming
- outline the needs of each type of farming to make it successful.

### Key vocabulary

- agriculture
- arable farming
- pastoral farming
- mixed farming
- relief
- climate
- crofting

### Skills builder

The spread asks pupils to sort through information and categorise it. The ability to skim read a section of text and extract the relevant information is an important tool. Pupils need to identify the key word that they are looking for and develop a pattern of skim reading – either side-to-side, top-to-bottom or a zigzag – to ensure that they find all examples of the word. They then need to read the rest of the sentence in more detail to determine if this is the relevant text needed to answer the question.

### Further discussion suggestions

- Which region does your school fall in?
- What type of farming do you see in your region?
- What factors influence the farming in your region?

### Answers to activities

1. Arable farming is when the land is ploughed and crops are grown.

   Pastoral farming is when grass is grown for the grazing of animals.

   Mixed farming is when animals are reared and crops grown in the same place.

2. The statements can fit into a number of the different farming types. An indication of the correct answer is found in the table below.

| Farming type | Description | Needs |
|---|---|---|
| Arable | Grows crops | Flat or gently sloping land<br>Fertile Soil<br>Modern machinery |
| Cattle | Produces milk and beef | Flat or gently sloping land<br>Warm, wet climate<br>Modern machinery |
| Hill Sheep | Produces wool, lamb and mutton | Hilly land<br>Little machinery<br>Any climate |
| Mixed | Raises animals and grows crops | Flat or gently sloping land<br>Fertile soil<br>Modern machinery<br>Warm, wet climate |

# 2 Economic activity

**Pupil Book pages 32–33**

# What is a hill sheep farm like?
# What is an arable farm like?

## About this spread

In this spread the pupils are asked to study small, traditional sheep farms, such as Beckside Farm, which are limited by the relief and climate. These businesses use little machinery in the production of wool, lamb and some crops such as oats, barley and turnips. The pupils contrast this with the large scale agribusinesses involved in the production of arable crops at Hawthorn Farm in East Anglia. Farms like this invest heavily in new farming methods and machinery to make the process as efficient as possible.

## Learning outcomes

By the end of this spread pupils should be able to:

- describe the location of different farms in the United Kingdom
- list the similarities and differences between hill farming and arable farming.

## Learning objectives

On this spread pupils should learn:

- where the different types of farming are located
- to compare and contrast hill sheep and arable farming.

## Skills builder

This spread gives the opportunity for pupils to attempt a description of a location. When describing a location it is best to use as many of the 4 'Ds' (data, density, direction and distance) as possible. The locator map in Activity 1 only gives pupils data in the form of location and direction to create their description with. If pupils have access to an atlas then they may also be able to comment on distance between the farms or distance to other features, such as the Pennines.

## Further discussion suggestions

- Why is there no arable farming in the north-west of the United Kingdom or sheep farming in East Anglia?
- What environmental issues might each type of farming create?

## Answers to activities

1. Beckside Farm is located in the Lake District which is in the north-west of England in the county of Cumbria. It is close to the Irish Sea to the west, Pennine Hills to the east and the Southern Uplands to the north.

   Hawthorn Farm is located to the east of the United Kingdom in the East Anglia region. It is in the county of Norfolk. It is close to the Fens to the west and the North Sea to the East.

2. 

|  | Hill sheep farm | Arable farm |
| --- | --- | --- |
| Location | A remote upland area. | An area of flat and generally accessible land. |
| Relief | High fells and steep, rocky hillsides with some use of the lower slopes for growing winter feed. | Gently sloping and low-lying. |
| Soils | Upland areas have poor soils supporting rough grasses. The soils lower down are deeper but often wet and difficult to cultivate. | Deep, fertile and well-drained so it is easy to grow crops. |
| Temperature | Summers are cool and winters are cold. | Warm summers and cold winters. |
| Precipitation | Heavy rainfall with snow in the winter. | Dry summers – rain falls mostly in the growing season. |
| Machinery | Difficult to use tractors and other heavy machinery on the high ground as it is inaccessible and often wet. | A lot. Tractors, combine harvesters, muck spreaders, sprayers, ploughs, seed drills and grain driers. |
| Transport | The remote location far from the main transport network means it takes longer to transport livestock. | Close to main roads to get product to market quickly. |
| Markets | Lambs and sheep are sold in local markets. | Sells wheat to make bread and other bakery products. |
| Difficulties | Poor climate, waterlogged soils and low incomes. | Flooding, summer thunderstorms, frost. |
| Source of Income | Money from selling lambs and sheep. Wool is also sold but does not make much money. | Selling crops as part of an agribusiness which provides money to invest in the farm. |

# 2 Economic activity

**Pupil Book pages 34–35**

**What is the best site for a factory? Choosing the right site – the iron and steel industry**

## About this spread

In this spread pupils are introduced to key words associated with manufacturing industry. Pupils are then given an example of a secondary industry in the United Kingdom. They are asked to examine one specific factory in South Wales and investigate the inputs and outputs that are needed to run the factory. The source of inputs and location of deliveries have changed over time and pupils will have an appreciation of what these changes are.

## Learning objectives

On this spread pupils should learn:

- how to define the key terms associated with the manufacturing industry
- how to understand the factors that help to locate an iron and steel works
- how to analyse a photo.

## Learning outcomes

By the end of this spread pupils should be able to:

- provide definitions for words such as 'market'
- explain why Port Talbot has a steel works
- research a factory close to where they live and identify the locational factors.

## Key vocabulary

- factory
- raw materials
- power
- labour
- transport
- market
- site
- industrialised

## Skills builder

Being able to interpret photos is an important skill in geography and in this spread pupils have the chance to practise these skills. In the photo there are a range of features that can be identified and this then links with the skill of diagram creation. Pupils can use the example provided to add annotations from the text or photo and give a complete picture of the factors that determine where to build an iron and steel works.

## Further discussion suggestions

- Would a new iron and steel works be built in the United Kingdom?
- How would the location of a high-tech industry, such as mobile phones, differ from an iron and steel works.

## Answers to activities

1 By matching up the key sentences you should get the following answers.

   **Raw materials** Natural resources from which goods are made.

   **Power** Needed to work the machines.

   **Labour** People who work in the factories.

   **Market** A place where manufactured goods are sold.

   **Transport** Needed to move raw materials, workers and goods.

   **Site** Where the factory is built.

2 **Raw materials** The steel works needs coke/coal, iron ore and limestone. Originally these products were found close by in the valleys of South Wales but are now imported.

   **Site** The steel works is on flat land, as a large factory is needed. It is close to the sea where docks were built allowing the raw materials to be unloaded straight into the factory.

   **Power** The steel works uses electricity, which comes from the National Grid.

   **Labour** The steel works needs a large number of skilled workers who live close to the steelworks. Nearby Swansea provides this work force.

   **Market** Sheet steel is produced and is used in the car industry in England.

   **Transport** The M4 motorway is close to the steel works that links South Wales with England. There are also railway lines for carrying heavy products. Ships are used to import raw materials to the steel works dock.

3 The factory chosen will vary but the headings used in Activity 2 can be used to structure the pupil's answer.

## 2 Economic activity

**Pupil Book pages 36–37**

# Choosing the right site – the car industry

### About this spread

On this spread pupils learn about the best sites for the car industry. Car assembly plants are an example of an industry that locates near to large urban areas – these provide both the necessary workforce and a potential market for the cars produced. The car industry provides a contrast to the iron and steel industry that pupils studied on pages 34–35, which began as a typical 19th-century industry locating as close as possible to the source of its raw materials.

### Learning outcomes

By the end of this spread pupils should be able to:

- describe the distribution pattern of the UK's car industry
- give reasons why car assembly plants locate close to large urban areas
- explain why Burnaston is a good site for a car factory.

### Key vocabulary

- **assemble**

### Learning objectives

On this spread pupils should learn:

- why car assembly plants locate close to large urban areas
- why Toyota chose Burnaston as the site for its assembly plant.

### Skills builder

Throughout their study of geography, pupils will need to use maps at a variety of scales in order to interpret physical and human landscapes. The OS maps used are most likely to be at scales of 1 : 25,000 or 1 : 50,000. The map of Burnaston included on this spread is a 1 : 50,000 map, which has textboxes added to help pupils understand why Toyota chose Burnaston as the site of its assembly plant. Encourage pupils to really analyse the OS maps they use. They provide a wealth of information in terms of both human and physical geography, not to mention history.

### Further discussion suggestions

- How can local authorities and central government encourage a major foreign car manufacturer to build its new factory at a particular location within the UK?
- What is a car assembly line? Where was this method of manufacture invented?
- Why did the Japanese tsunami of 2011 disrupt car manufacture in the UK?

### Answers to activities

1. 
   - Cars are assembled from many small parts.
   - Cars need a big local market.
   - Cars are assembled near big cities.
   - Most cars are assembled in the West Midlands.

2. Reasons include:
   - Large towns provide a market.
   - Large towns provide a workforce.
   - Large towns have good transport links for moving around car parts, assembled cars and the workforce.

3. Advantages include:
   - Components are supplied to the assembly line minutes before they are needed.
   - Parts do not have to be stored on site.
   
   Disadvantages include:
   - Suppliers will be under pressure to deliver at the right time.
   - It relies on a good transport system.

4. Pupils' fact files should include the following information.

   **Burnaston car factory**

   **Raw materials** Many components are made in local factories and are delivered 'just-in-time'.

   **Power** Electricity is supplied through the National Grid.

   **Labour** Many skilled workers live in the local area; the attractive countryside and pleasant villages will attract workers to the area to work at the factory.

   **Markets** The factory is close to the large town of Derby and other large centres of population; cars are also sold in Europe and even Japan.

   **Transport** There are good road and rail links for the transport of components to the factory and finished cars to major UK markets; there is good access by road to the major ports for export markets.

   **Site** The site is large and flat with room for expansion.

# 2 Economic activity

**Pupil Book pages 38–39**

# What is the tourist industry?

## About this spread

This spread introduces tourism and how tourism has grown between 1950 and 2012. It also suggests some of the reasons why tourism might have grown between those dates. The importance of tourism to the economy is examined and some of the jobs provided by tourism are revealed. The spread also invites pupils to consider the positive and negative effects of a tourist development to both the local people and the natural environment that the development is located.

## Learning objectives

On this spread pupils should learn:

- how tourist numbers have changed through time
- about the importance of tourism in the economy of a tourist region
- that there are advantages and disadvantages to a tourist development.

## Learning outcomes

By the end of this spread pupils should be able to:

- describe how the number of world tourists has changed
- list the types of job associated with tourism
- consider both sides of the argument.

## Key vocabulary

- tourist/tourism
- standard of living

## Skills builder

Describing a graph is a skill that is tested in this spread. The first point to make is the overall trend of the data – is there an increase or a decrease from the start of the graph to the finish? The second point to consider is the rate of change – does the graph show a smooth and consistent increase or are there increases and decreases? Are there large jumps between different points on the graph? The final point to comment on is whether there are any anomalies. If the question asks you to describe then you do not need to provide an explanation.

## Further discussion suggestions

- What effect might the financial crisis have had on the number of tourists?
- How much do LEDCs benefit from a tourist development?

## Answers to activities

1. The graph shows that there has been an increase in the number of tourists from around 50 million in 1950 to 1,050 million in 2012.

   It is not a steady increase, with smaller increases in the early years.

   Between 1950 and 1960 there was an increase of 15 million. Larger increases occurred between 1990 and 2010 with the largest of around 300 million between 1990 and 2000.

2. Answers could be in a similar style to the one below.

   a  I would prefer to be a ski instructor because it would involve being on the ski slopes teaching beginners how to ski and skiing is one of my favourite activities. I would also be outside in a beautiful location with lovely mountainous scenery.

   b  Fifteen jobs could include: chambermaid, waiter, lifeguard, policeman, watersports instructor, children's club rep, tourist information officer, nightclub owner, singer, air steward, hotel receptionist, taxi transfer driver, beach cleaner, hotel maintenance man, nightclub bouncer.

3. Three reasons to be in favour of the plan could include the following.

   - It would bring more jobs to the area for local people and increase the standard of living.
   - There would be an increase in the number of facilities that locals can use, such as restaurants.
   - Money could be spent on older buildings which may need repair.
   - The increased revenue brought in by tourists could be used to improve the quality of the environment by enabling new schools, hospitals and roads to be built.

   Three reasons to be against the plan could include the following.

   - There would be increased levels of noise disturbing local people.
   - The amount of litter would increase making the area look untidy.
   - Prices will rise so that local people can't afford to live there.
   - The possibility of an increase in the crime rate makes people feel unsafe.
   - Any jobs created are likely to be seasonal and poorly paid.
   - Possibility of local customs and traditions would be lost.

# 2 Economic activity

**Pupil Book pages 40–41**

# Where do the tourists go?

## About this spread

In this spread pupils can see the spatial variation in tourist arrivals between the continents. It also highlights the top destinations in both number of tourists and the amount of money that they make. Pupils are asked to consider the different types of holiday destination and what type of tourist is likely to be attracted to each area. They are also given the opportunity to practise justifying decisions they have made.

## Learning objectives

On this spread pupils should learn:

- to interpret information provided on tourist destinations
- to make a decision on a type of holiday for one group of people and provide reasons for the destination chosen.

## Learning outcomes

By the end of this spread pupils should be able to:

- identify the most popular tourist resorts in the world
- justify a decision about where someone should go on holiday
- use a computer to research different types of holiday.

## Skills builder

A skill that this spread seeks pupils to practise is that of justification. Pupils are given a certain scenario and then asked to suggest a type of holiday that might appeal to that group. The actual choice that the pupil makes is not particularly important, what matters is their justification for the decision that they have made. Each idea should be explained fully and each idea fully explored before moving on to a different reason. To increase the complexity you could ask pupils to explain which reason was the one they consider to be most important and why it is more important than any other reason.

## Further discussion suggestions

- Why is there such a disparity in tourist arrivals between the different continents?
- Do local people always want tourists?

## Answers to activities

**1 a** The correct order is:

Europe, 51.7%
East Asia and Pacific, 19.6%
North America, 9.9%
Middle East, 5.4%
Africa, 4.8%
Caribbean, 3.1%
South America, 2.7%
South Asia/Oceania, 1.4% each.

**b** Europe was the most visited continent by 32.1%

**c** The tourist industry is long established in Europe. Reasons could include a wide range of attractions including beaches, historic buildings, theme parks and the natural scenery. It could also include factors such as a wealthy population and good transport links including a good road network, rail connections and airports. A further set of factors could include access to technology which makes it faster and more convenient to research and book holidays online.

**2** A pupil's answers could include:

- Famous buildings: Paris (Eiffel Tower, Arc de Triomphe)
- New cultures: Thailand (Buddhist culture)
- Beach resorts: Spain (Costa Brava)
- City breaks: Slovenia (Ljubljana)
- River/ocean cruises: Central Europe (The Danube)
- Wildlife: Safari in Kenya (Masai Mara)
- Works of art: St Petersburg (The Winter Palace or The Hermitage)
- Different foods: South Korea (kimchi)
- Ski resorts: Canada (Whistler, Banff)
- Theme parks: USA (Disneyland, Florida)
- Spectacular scenery: United Kingdom (Lake District)
- Better climate: Portugal (Algarve)

**3 a** A pupil's answer could include:

I would suggest a beach resort in Majorca for a family with three young children. This would be a good place to visit as it is relatively cheap for a large group. It is a short flight which will stop the children getting too bored. Most hotels have a kids' club which means that the parents can have a break with the children being looked after. There will also be a swimming pool and other sporting facilities which will help keep the children entertained. The beach is a place children usually enjoy and the sand is good for sandcastles. The sea does not have strong tides and is generally safe for swimming.

**b** A pupil's answer could include:

I would suggest a Mediterranean cruise for a retired couple. They would be based on the cruise ship meaning they don't need to worry about accommodation or food as these are provided. There is entertainment on the ship so if the couple doesn't want to leave the ship they don't have to. The cruise will take them to several destinations offering different places to investigate without having to worry about the transport links. The cities that they visit often have a historic heart with art galleries and museums that might interest the retired couple.

**4** Pupils' answers will vary. See the previous answer for an example of the level of detail that pupils could provide.

## 2 Economic activity

**Pupil Book pages 42–43**

# What are high-tech industries?

### About this spread

This spread and pages 44–45 look at high-tech industries and what they are – they make products such as microchips, computers, mobile phones, pharmaceuticals and scientific equipment. It looks at location and the fact that these industries are frequently grouped together on science or business parks which are often located on greenfield sites on the edge of cities.

### Learning objectives

On this spread pupils should learn:

- that high-tech industries make products using advanced scientific techniques
- that companies making high-tech products often locate together on science and business parks.

### Learning outcomes

By the end of this spread pupils should be able to:

- explain what high-tech industries are
- describe the differences between a science park and a business park
- give reasons why a high-tech industry should locate on a science park.

### Key vocabulary

- high-tech industry
- science park
- business park
- greenfield site

### Skills builder

Pupils need to be encouraged to always read and fully understand the question or activity that they are being asked to do, so that they can answer to the best of their ability. They should be aware of the importance of command words in the activities such as 'describe', 'explain', 'name', and so on. In the activities on this spread, pupils are asked to do a range of different things.

- In Activity 1a they need to explain what high-tech industries are and in 1b to name high-tech products.
- In Activity 2 they complete a table using the words provided.
- In Activity 3 they use a photo and a diagram to give reasons why high-tech firms should locate on a science park. They should include words they have been given.
- In Activity 4 they are asked to give two disadvantages of firms locating in the same place.

### Further discussion suggestions

- Why are high-tech industries known as 'sunrise' industries?
- What impact does information technology have on your daily life?
- What are microprocessors and microchips?

### Answers to activities

1. **a** High-tech industries are those that make use of the most advanced technology available. Products include those such as microchips, computers, mobile phones, pharmaceutical products and scientific equipment.

   **b** Pupils should name five high-tech products they have used in the last week. The products they name will vary, but should match the types of products listed in Activity 1a.

2. 
|   | Science park | Business park |
|---|---|---|
| a | very few | many |
| b | university links | No university links |
| c | high-tech firms | high-tech firms, shops, hotels, leisure centres |

3. Pupils' answers will vary, but they should be similar to the answer below and include the terms given in bold.

   Science parks are located on the edge of a city where the **price of land** is cheaper than in the city centre. Science parks should be near to a main road to provide good **transport** links. The edge-of-city location provides a pleasant, clean **environment** with grassy areas, ornamental gardens, lakes and ponds, which is good for **people's health**. The large site means that **leisure facilities** can be provided for the people who work there. Being on the same site as other high-tech firms means it is easy to **exchange ideas with people from other firms**.

4. Pupils are asked to give two disadvantages. These can be taken from the disadvantages given on page 43 of the pupil book.

   - Over-use of cars can cause traffic congestion at busy times.
   - Edge-of-town sites can be far from shops and services.
   - Firms may prefer to locate on their own to keep new ideas secret.
   - It may be difficult for firms to find enough skilled workers.

## 2 Economic activity

### Pupil Book pages 44–45: Where are high-tech industries located?

#### About this spread

This spread follows on from pages 42–43 and looks in more detail at the location of high-tech industries. Unlike the old traditional industries, such as iron and steelmaking, which had to locate closer to raw materials and markets, high-tech industries have a much freer choice of location. Despite this, three areas of Britain have become particularly important: the M4 corridor; 'Silicon Glen' in central Scotland; and 'Silicon Fen' around Cambridge.

#### Learning outcomes

By the end of this spread pupils should be able to:

- complete a sketch to show what makes a good site for a high-tech factory
- understand that high-tech industries are not tied to a particular location in the same way that old traditional industries had been
- explain why the M4 corridor is a good location for a high-tech industries.

#### Key vocabulary

- sunset industries
- sunrise industries

#### Learning objectives

On this spread pupils should learn:

- about the factors that affect the location of high-tech industries
- that there are three main areas in Britain where high-tech industries have located.

#### Skills builder

This chapter includes theoretical aspects of industrial location, e.g. the best sites for a factory, choosing a site for the iron and steel industry and the car industry, and where high-tech industries are located. It also aims to link the theory to actual examples of industrial location. So, it includes the iron and steel industry in Port Talbot, the Toyota factory in Burnaston and high-tech industries along the M4 corridor. The inclusion of modern industries should help pupils to see that geography is a real subject relevant to the contemporary world around them.

#### Further discussion suggestions

- Why are high-tech industries sometimes referred to as 'footloose' industries?
- Why are so many UK high-tech industries located close to the M4 motorway and Heathrow airport?
- What makes business and science parks such attractive places in which to work?

#### Answers to activities

1. Sunset industries are those that are in decline. They include industries such as shipbuilding, steelmaking, chemical manufacture and textiles. Sunrise industries are growth industries. They include high-tech industries that use modern factories.

2. **a**, **b** and **c**

   Pupils' sketches should look similar to this.

   Yellow: near to motorways, motorway junctions and main roads for good communications and transport links

   Brown: close to universities (not shown) for research facilities and a source of qualified and skilled workers

   Green: on the edge of town near attractive countryside and open space, which provides a pleasant environment for people to work in

   Red: near nice housing to attract workers to the industries

   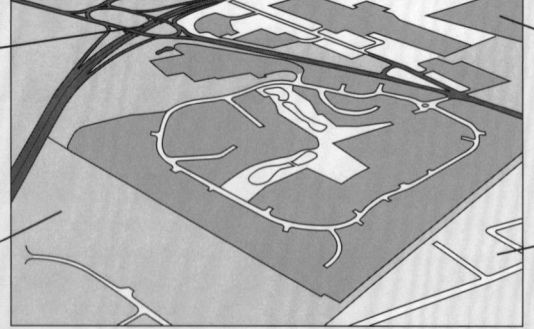

3. The M4 corridor is a good location for high-tech industries because:

   - it has good transport links – it is close to other motorways and Heathrow Airport (for international links), and also other airports including Bristol, Gatwick and Stansted
   - there are four university cities/towns relatively close to the M4 (Bristol, Oxford, Reading and London), which will provide highly qualified and skilled workers and research facilities within the universities
   - it runs through, and is close to, a number of upland areas with open space and attractive countryside, which will be attractive to workers.

# 2 Economic activity

**Pupil Book pages 46–47**

# The economic activity enquiry

## About this spread

This economic activity enquiry brings together a range of different skills and concepts from throughout the chapter. It also relies on map work and photo interpretation so it may be worth refreshing those skills using chapter 6 of the pupil book and also chapters 6 and 7 from *Nelson Key Geography Foundations*. It is one of four enquiries in the pupil book and provides an opportunity to assess pupils' progress.

## Learning outcomes

By the end of this spread pupils should be able to:

- use the map to practise reading heights and using grid references
- prioritise the attractions that appeal to the pupil
- draw conclusions and display them in a sketch map format.

## How can enquiries help with assessment?

For each enquiry in *Connections* there is a checklist in the appendices. The checklist provides pupils with success criteria so that they know what is expected in order to produce high-quality answers and improve in the future. The checklist can be used in two ways.

- Pupils can use these as they go along, to check that they are meeting the success criteria for the enquiry.
- They can be used for assessment either by you, as the teacher, or another pupil, for peer marking. Any element that is not ticked provides evidence that the pupil has not met all of the criteria.

## Learning objectives

On this spread pupils should learn:

- to interpret a map and a photo to assess if Porthcawl is the right place for a holiday.

## What is the economic activity enquiry about?

This enquiry builds on the work pupils have done earlier in this unit on industrial location. The pupils' task is to draw up a list of the attractions that their ideal coastal tourist resort would have and then apply them to the information provided in the map and photo of Porthcawl.

The enquiry should include:

- a copy of table A from page 46, completed by listing the physical and human attractions that an ideal resort would have so that the pupils can identify what they are looking for.
- a copy of table C from page 47, answering the questions to help practise using map skills.
- use the map and photo to compare Porthcawl to the attractions in their ideal resort
- make a sketch map of map B on page 46 and label it to show the pupils' conclusions.

## Differentiation suggestions

*For lower-ability pupils*

- Work with pupils to make sure they are clear about the steps they need to go through in order to complete the enquiry.
- Use chapter 6 from *Connections* and also chapters 6 and 7 in *Foundations* to help pupils refresh their map skills.
- You could provide pupils with the start of a sketch of map B from page 46 (e.g. the some of the coastline and some of the major features), so that pupils understand how they should annotate the map.
- Provide the start to each label and ask the student to complete it.

*For higher-ability pupils*

Ask pupils to find their own tourist resort. After sourcing their own maps and photos they could follow a similar structure to that outlined in this enquiry. It could be in another country and instead of using a beach area, it could be a different type of holiday destination e.g. a historic town or a National Park.

Make the command question a little more challenging, examples could be 'Assess the relative importance of the different factors bringing tourists to Porthcawl' or 'Produce a plan to increase the number of tourists visiting Porthcawl. Use the map and photo to justify the reasons for your plan.'

# 3 Population

**Pupil Book pages 50–51**

## Are we spread evenly?

### About this spread

This spread introduces pupils to the idea of population distribution (how people are spread out) and population density (how crowded places are). It looks at the population distribution of the UK, and the importance of towns and cities as places to live (80 per cent of the UK's population live in urban areas). The spread ends by asking pupils why they think some places are crowded, while other places have very few people living there.

### Learning outcomes

By the end of this spread pupils should be able to:

- define the terms 'population distribution' and 'population density'
- describe the distribution of population across Britain
- identify reasons why some places are densely populated, while others are sparsely populated.

### Key vocabulary

- population distribution
- population density
- densely populated
- sparsely populated

### Learning objectives

On this spread pupils should learn:

- that the population of the UK is not evenly distributed
- the reasons why some places, such as cities, are densely populated, while others are sparsely populated.

### Skills builder

Using maps is a key geographical skill. Pupils need to be able to identify patterns and describe distributions shown on maps. The text and activities on this spread, together with the map of the population distribution of the UK, enables pupils to see quite clearly that people are not evenly distributed across the UK. The south and east are most crowded; and the north and west are least crowded.

Choropleth maps use different colours or shading to show differences between places and distributions, as the population distribution map shows on page 50. More help on choropleth maps can be found on pages 112 and 113.

### Further discussion suggestions

What are the advantages and disadvantages of living in London?

- What makes young people leave the sparsely populated countryside to live in a densely populated town?
- How do road transport links affect the distribution of population in the UK?

### Answers to activities

1. **a** A **population distribution** map shows how people are spread out across the country.

   **b** **Population density** tells us how crowded places are.

   **c** **Densely populated** means that places are crowded; they have a high population density.

   **d** **Sparsely populated** means that places have few people; they have a low population density.

2. **a** Pupils should copy map F and complete a key, which will be the same as the key for map A.

   **b** Pupils' paragraphs should include the words in the textbox (shown in **bold** below), and should be similar to the following.

   Britain's population is **unevenly spread** out. The **south** and **east** are the most **densely** populated areas. The **north** and **west** are the most **sparsely** populated areas.

3. **a** The cities in order of size are (biggest first): London, Birmingham, Leeds, Glasgow, Liverpool, Edinburgh, Manchester, Bristol, Cardiff, Belfast, Newcastle, Southampton.

   **b** Pupils are asked for three advantages of living in cities. These include: being close to other people; being close to shops; being close to jobs; being close to entertainment.

4. **a** People live in cities such as that shown in photo D because cities provide jobs, homes, shops, entertainment and plenty of opportunities for other activities.

   **b** Few people live in areas like that shown in photo E because there are few jobs in these areas, few shops or homes and little in the way of entertainment and social activity compared with towns and cities.

5.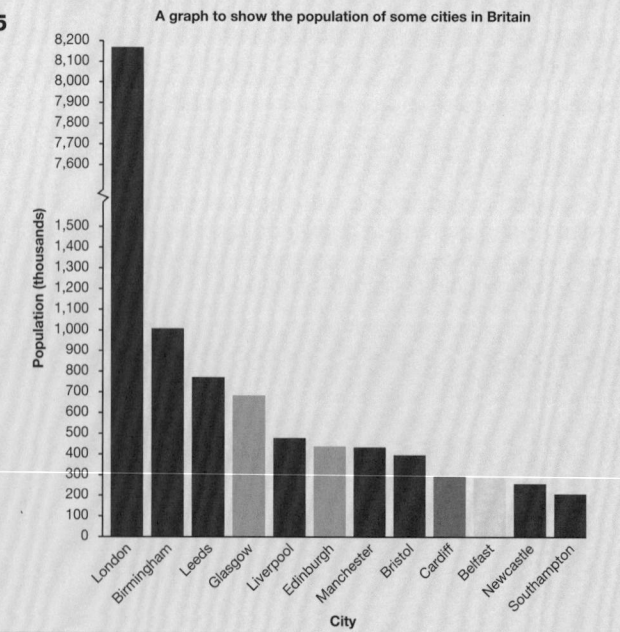

# 3 Population

**Pupil Book pages 52–53**

# What affects where we live?

## About this spread

This spread looks at why few people live in some areas and many people live in others. This is introduced through the use of photos. This is then followed by the possible negative factors that discourage people from living in certain areas, and positive factors that encourage people to live in others.

## Learning outcomes

By the end of this spread pupils should be able to:

- understand that the world's population distribution is affected by many things, including relief, climate, vegetation, water supply, raw materials and employment opportunities
- give examples of negative factors (which result in sparse population) and positive factors (which result in dense population).

## Key vocabulary

- negative factors
- water supply
- positive factors

## Learning objectives

On this spread pupils should learn:

- that the world's population is unevenly distributed
- that negative factors discourage people from settling in some places
- that positive factors encourage people to settle in other places.

## Skills builder

This spread uses six photos to illustrate negative and positive factors that either discourage or encourage people to settle in different areas. The activities enable pupils to analyse the photos by matching some to different words and phrases and asking pupils to list words and phrases for others. A large number of photos are included in the *Key Geography* books. They have all been carefully briefed and chosen to fulfil a specific purpose. Consequently, pupils should learn to use them and interpret what they show, and sometimes draw sketches from them and annotate them. Note that chapter 7 in *Nelson Key Geography Foundations* is dedicated to using photos.

## Further discussion suggestions

- Why does most of Japan's population live on or near the coast?
- Where we live affects how we live. What does this mean?
- Does our happiness depend on where and how we live?

## Answers to activities

1. **a** Photo A – Himalayan Mountains.
   **b** level, wet, good farming, hot.
   **c** Pupils' answers will vary, but they should include at least eight different things to describe photo D.

2. 

| Sparsely populated (negative factors) | Densely populated (positive factors) |
|---|---|
| Mountains | Flat land |
| Dense forest | Lowland |
| Unreliable water supply | Open grassland |
| Thin, poor soils | Good farming |
| Poor farming | Deep, rich soils |
| Deserts | Job opportunities |

3. **a** Reasons include: steep slopes; poor soils; little industry; few jobs.
   **b** Reasons include: poor/no soils; very hot; very dry; poor water supply; little industry; few jobs.

4. Pupils' answers will vary. A possible answer could be something like:

   Where I live is a densely populated area. This is because it has a pleasant climate with an average temperature of 19 °C and rainfall of about 1000 mm a year. These are good conditions for crops grow well, which provides a lot of food, meaning that more people live in the area. There are gentle slopes and no mountains making it easy to build large towns and cities which leads to a higher population density.

   Other factors could include: access to good healthcare; education; transport network; and communications or easy access to entertainment.

# 3 Population

## Pupil Book pages 54–55
## Where do we live?

### About this spread

This spread is concerned with the global distribution of population and looks at why some parts of the world are very sparsely populated, while other parts contain very large numbers of people. The photo-map on page 54 is an image of the earth from space, as seen by the NOAA satellite orbiting 830 km above the earth's surface. The photo mosaic clearly shows some of the world's features. Some of these can be linked to the distribution of population, which has been added to the original photo as an overlay of red dots. The rapid growth of cities in some of the world's poorer countries is covered on page 55.

### Learning objectives

On this spread pupils should learn:
- about the global distribution of population
- about the distribution of the world's fastest-growing cities.

### Skills builder

Activity 6 requires pupils to use an atlas. They need to find out in which countries the world's fastest-growing cities shown on map B are located. They can do this either by using a world map in an atlas or by using the index in the atlas. In Activity 7, pupils need to look at atlas maps of Australia and the USA and interpret what they show. The map of Australia will show that the central part consists of desert and land over 1,000 m. It is too hot, dry and, in some areas, the land is too high for people to settle there. The map of the USA should show pupils that the east coast and south-west USA are low-lying compared with much of the USA, and will therefore be more densely populated than the rest of the country.

### Learning outcomes

By the end of this spread pupils should be able to:
- understand why people are not spread evenly over the world
- give examples of densely populated and sparsely populated areas
- describe the distribution of the world's fastest-growing cities
- give reasons why people live in cities.

### Further discussion suggestions

- Why do the world's fastest-growing cities tend to be in poorer countries?
- Monaco, situated between France and Italy on the Mediterranean coast, is the most densely populated country in the world, although its population is only 37,300. Why is it so densely populated?

### Answers to activities

1. 
   a. The distribution of population over the world is **uneven**.
   b. The areas with the fewest people are the dense forests, **deserts** and **polar regions**.
   c. Mountainous areas are **sparsely** populated.
   d. Areas with good resources and industry are **densely** populated.

2. 
   a. Densely populated areas include Western Europe, India, China, Japan and Bangladesh. Pupils are asked to name four areas, so could include others indicated on map A.
   b. Sparsely populated areas include the Amazon rainforest, Himalayan mountains, polar regions (Arctic and Antarctic), Sahara Desert (and other desert areas). Pupils should name six sparsely populated areas, and could include other areas indicated on map A.

3. 
   a. São Paulo is the only city in South America.
   b. Karachi, Delhi, Mumbai (Bombay), Kolkata (Calcutta), Dhaka, Jakarta, Seoul and Tokyo are all in Asia.
   c. Tokyo is in Japan, a rich country.

4. They provide housing / They provide medical care / They provide education / They provide entertainment / They provide jobs / They provide opportunities to 'get on' and improve people's lives → Why cities are popular

5. The ten fastest-growing cities are:
   - mainly in poor countries
   - mainly between the tropics
   - in South America and Asia.

6. The cities are in the following countries:
   1. Mexico City, Mexico
   2. São Paulo, Brazil
   3. Karachi, Pakistan
   4. Delhi, India
   5. Mumbai, India
   6. Kolkata, India
   7. Dhaka, Bangladesh
   8. Jakarta, Indonesia
   9. Seoul, South Korea
   10. Tokyo, Japan

7. Central Australia is sparsely populated because it has a harsh climate. The temperature in the summer can be warmer than 40 °C and in some months the rainfall can be as low as 9 mm. This makes it difficult to grow crops and provide food for people. With few communities it means that there aren't enough roads or rails links, which makes it harder to live there.

   The east coast of the USA is densely populated because it is close to the coast. Cities such as New York and Boston have large ports where goods can be imported and exported. This provides jobs in shipping and other related industries. This means that there is a high population density as people tend to live close to where they work. Other industries such as retail and entertainment will start to provide services for the workers. This will help to increase the population density of the area. The south-west has advantages such as the climate and proximity to the high-tech industry of Silicon Valley near San Francisco. These factors, as well as the high standard of living, makes living and working in the area an attractive proposition.

# 3 Population

**Pupil Book pages 56–57**

# How does population change?

## About this spread

This spread covers aspects of population change and growth. The relatively recent huge and rapid increase in the world's population – called a population explosion – is considered to be one of the world's biggest problems and graph A shows this dramatic increase. These pages explain what the terms 'birth rate' and 'death rate' mean and how they cause populations to change. The difference between birth and death rates gives the natural increase in population, and table E shows how birth and death rates vary between countries along with the resulting differences in population growth.

## Learning outcomes

By the end of this spread pupils should be able to:

- define the terms 'birth rate', 'death rate' and 'population growth rate'
- describe the growth in the world's population since the early 1800s
- understand that population growth is much faster in poorer countries than in richer ones.

## Key vocabulary

- population explosion
- birth rate
- death rate
- population growth rate

## Learning objectives

On this spread pupils should learn:

- about the rapid increase in the world's population
- about some of the factors influencing birth and death rates in different parts of the world.

## Skills builder

There is a lot of subject-specific terminology and key vocabulary for pupils to get to grips with in some geographical topics, and this is true of population. Pupils will achieve at a higher level if they are able to use the correct terminology. You could help them by displaying key words and their meanings around the classroom. Pupils could also be asked to complete a dictionary of key vocabulary for this unit, as has been suggested for other units. The glossary at the end of the pupil book will help them.

## Further discussion suggestions

- Why do couples in developed countries generally have fewer children than couples in developing countries?
- Why did China try to restrict the growth of its population with the one-child policy?
- Russia has the second-highest death rate in the world, and a low birth rate, so the population is declining. What effect will this have on the country's economy?

## Answers to activities

**1 a** 1820

 **b** 110 years

 **c** 44 years

**2** The world's population rose slowly between the years 1100 and 1650. Between 1650 and 1820, there was an increase in the rate of population growth as the world's population doubled from 500 million to 1,000 million (1 billion). Since 1820, the world's population has grown at a faster rate, with an 'explosion' from about 1930 onwards.

**3 a**
- Birth rate is the number of babies born each year per 1,000 population.
- Death rate is the number of people who die each year per 1,000 population.
- Population growth rate is the speed at which the population increases.

 **b** 'Explosion' is a good term to use because population has grown so fast.

**4**

| Births | Deaths | Population change |
|---|---|---|
| ↗ | → | Increase |
| → | ↗ | Decrease |
| → | → | Same |
| ↗ | ↗ | Same |

**5 a** Countries listed in size of natural increase (greatest increase first): Bangladesh; Mexico; India; Brazil; China; USA; France; UK; Italy; Japan.

 **b** The richer countries have lower rates of natural increase than poorer countries. In poorer countries the rate of natural increase is seven or more per 1,000. In richer countries the rate of natural increase is below seven per 1,000.

**6** The table shows the most common answer but many of them can be put in multiple columns – for instance, war will lead to a high death rate as many people die, but as it is mainly men sent to fight this splits up families and can reduce the birth rate.

| Birth Rate | | Death Rate | |
|---|---|---|---|
| High | Low | High | Low |
| Traditions for larger families | Birth Control available | Food shortages | New hospitals |
| Children needed to help with work | | Poor health care | Improved water supply |
| | | War | Good harvest |

**7** Three reasons could include any of the following or the pupil's own valid choice:

- better diet
- better quality health care
- improved sanitation
- improved hygiene

# 3 Population

**Pupil Book pages 58–59**

# What is migration?

## About this spread

This spread looks at the issue of migration and how this affects population change. It deals with what migration is and the push and pull factors that cause people to migrate.

## Learning objectives

On this spread pupils should learn:
- what migration is
- why people migrate.

## Learning outcomes

By the end of this spread pupils should be able to:
- define the terms 'migration', 'rural-to-urban migration' and 'international migration'
- give examples of push and pull factors
- understand that migration affects population size and the mix of people living in a place.

## Skills builder

Throughout their study of geography pupils will develop a range of skills, including graphical skills, and they need to be able to construct and interpret what different types of graphs show. In Activity 2, pupils are asked to complete a bar graph showing population growth in London. They are then asked to describe the changes shown on the graph and suggest reasons for the change.

## Key vocabulary

- migration
- migrants
- rural-to-urban migration
- international migration
- push factors
- pull factors

## Further discussion suggestions

- What is the bright-light syndrome and how does it affect migrants' lives?
- What are the benefits of migrants to an area?
- What are the disadvantages of migrants to an area?

## Answers to activities

1. 
   - Migration is the movement of people from one place to another.
   - Rural-to-urban migration is when people move from the countryside to towns and cities.
   - International migration is when people move from one country to another.

2. a Pupils' graphs should look like this.

   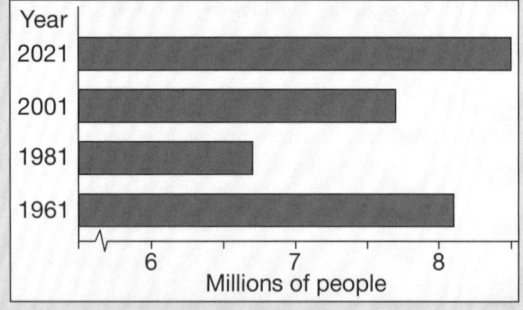

   b London's population declined significantly from 1961 to 1981. Since 1981, the population has increased and is estimated to continue increasing to 2021. Since 1981, the growth in population has been rapid.

   c The increase in London's population is partly the result of natural increase, but mainly because of migration.

3. a Note that pupils are asked to give two examples.

   A push factor is something that makes people migrate. They include: political fears; not enough jobs; few opportunities; natural disasters; wars; ethnic or religious persecution; unhappy lives; shortage of food; and poor living conditions.

   b Note that pupils are asked to give two examples.

   A pull factor is something that attracts people to a new place. They include: a better way of life; the chance of a job; improved living conditions; education; better housing; medical care; family links; and pleasant surroundings.

4. The factors that pupils identify and put in table F help to explain why the people in diagram C migrated to London.

| | Push factor | Pull factor |
|---|---|---|
| Hamish | Poor health | Family links, medical care |
| Janine | | Job/more experience, new friends |
| Carmel | | Family originally came for jobs |
| Caroline | | Better job |
| Chang | Sent by company for job | Way of life |
| Zaric | Family killed in Croatia, political fear | Safety, new life |

5. a This activity gives pupils an opportunity to produce a piece of extended writing and to be a bit creative. Their descriptions will vary, but they should include language issues, getting a job, food, shelter (housing), making friends, and so on.

   b Pupils' descriptions should include the fact that Zaric's family were killed in the war in Croatia and that he felt in danger (political fear is a push factor). He moved to London to start again: for a better life, the chance of a job, and so on (pull factors).

# 3 Population

**Pupil Book pages 60–61**

# Who migrates to the UK?

## About this spread

This spread continues with the theme of migration, but looks specifically at who migrates to the UK. Pupils are made aware of the fact that migration to the UK is nothing new – people have been arriving in Britain from other countries for over 2,000 years, and Britain has always been a place of mixed races and cultures. While in the 1950s many migrants to the UK came from countries that were once part of the British Empire. By the 1990s nearly 60 per cent of immigrants came from the EU. This spread also looks at asylum seekers and some of the issues raised by their arrival in the UK.

## Learning outcomes

By the end of this spread pupils should be able to:
- describe how the UK's population is made up
- describe where migrants to the UK are from.

## Key vocabulary

- immigrants
- asylum seekers

## Learning objectives

On this spread pupils should learn:
- about the role that immigration has played in the current population of the UK
- why different groups of people have migrated to the UK.

## Skills builder

In Activity 4 pupils are asked to write a letter to a newspaper supporting asylum seekers. This provides them with an opportunity to produce a slightly longer piece of writing than many of the activities require. They can also practise their written English. Their letter should include relevant information organised in a clear and coherent manner. They can use the information on Zaric on page 58 and graphs D on page 61 to help them. Pupils' spelling, punctuation and grammar should be accurate, and the style of writing should be appropriate for inclusion in a newspaper.

## Further discussion suggestions

- Citizens of the EU can move freely between member states to live and work. What impact might this have on the UK?
- What problems might arise if immigrants to a country can't speak the country's language?
- The number of people who immigrate to the UK is not balanced by the number of people who emigrate from the UK to other countries. Why not?

## Answers to activities

**1 a** Nineteen languages (if you include British sign language).

**b** Pupils can select any three European and three non-European welcome signs to write out. Check that they are correct in their selections of European and non-European.

**2** This activity will probably work best if done as a class activity. Pupils should use the headings 'Born in the UK' and 'Born outside the UK'. The latter should then be subdivided into 'Born in EU', 'Born in USA and Canada', and so on, using the headings from graph B on page 60.

**3 a** Most of the immigrants to the UK have come from the EU.

**b** The UK is a member of the EU and people from EU member states can move relatively freely and easily to work in other member states.

**c** Immigrants from India, Pakistan and Bangladesh are likely to have relatives in the UK already, as many people from these countries moved to fill job shortages after the Second World War.

**4** Pupils should use the information on Zaric, as well as figure D on page 61, to help write their letter supporting asylum seekers.

# 3 Population

**Pupil Book pages 62–63**

# What are the effects of migration?

## About this spread

Migration into Britain has meant an increase in population and has resulted in the multicultural society we have today. Migration also affects the migrants themselves, the places they move to, as well as the places they move from. This spread investigates some of these effects.

## Learning objectives

On this spread pupils should learn:

- about the effects of migration on different groups of people
- about the effects of migration on the countries they move to.

## Learning outcomes

By the end of this spread pupils should be able to:

- give reasons why some people might find migration difficult
- sort some of the effects of migration
- into advantages and disadvantages.

## Key vocabulary

- multicultural society

## Skills builder

Activity 2 asks pupils to arrange statements about migration in a diamond shape, i.e. a diamond grid. Geographers often need to put things in order. Ordering things like the population size of cities or the wealth of different countries is straightforward. Other things may be more difficult to put into a simple order and that is when a diamond grid can be useful. It allows you to group together things of a similar importance.

## Further discussion suggestions

- Many cities in the UK (and throughout the world) have a Chinatown with a distinctive character. Why is this?
- What effect does migration have on the countries that migrants have left?

## Answers to activities

1. **a** The Singh family are pleased they migrated to the UK because:

   - Sanjit got a job straight away in a clothing factory
   - they have a flat
   - the children are at the local school
   - they are learning the English language
   - they have made lots of friends.

   **b** The Khafoor family are unhappy about migrating to the UK because:

   - they can't speak the language very well
   - they have had difficulty finding work
   - they have had difficulty making friends
   - it has been hard for them to find a decent place to live, as they have little money and are getting little help
   - they are homesick.

2. Pupils' diamond grids will vary, as they are bound to have differing opinions about which is the most important advantage and which is the greatest disadvantage, and so on. Although the activity does not ask pupils to justify the position of their statements, it might be worth quizzing them to check their reasoning is sound.

3. Pupils are asked to give reasons for the headlines in artwork E and write a short newspaper article for each. Their reasons should be along the following lines.

   - **Newham News** Local businesses welcome migrants: immigrants may be young, skilled and hard working; immigrants may be happy to do the jobs that local people do not want to do.
   - **London Star** UK to restrict entry of migrants: migrants are accused of taking away people's jobs, putting a strain on services such as health and social services, etc.
   - **Daily Herald** Unions concerned over migrant rights: migrants may be forced to work for long hours for low pay.

   Pupils' articles should include the reasons they have identified for each headline, and any other information they think is useful from this spread.

## 3 Population

**Pupil Book pages 64–65**

# How can we compare local areas?

## About this spread

This unit is about people – where they live, how many there are and why people move from one place to another. This spread encourages pupils to look at areas at a local level and compare them in terms of their population. They are also encouraged to look at the population and people who live in their own local area and compare it with the UK. See the answers to Activity 3 for accessing information on the local area on the National Statistics website.

## Learning outcomes

By the end of this spread pupils should be able to:

- use statistical data to describe the differences between areas
- produce a report to compare the population of the local area with national averages.

## Learning objectives

On this spread pupils should learn:

- how to use statistical data to compare the population for different areas.

## Skills builder

The key skill that pupils will be building on this spread is the ability to use and interpret a range of graphs and statistics in order to compare two different areas in London. Pupils look at total population data, divided bar graphs showing people in different age groups, and pie graphs showing people from different ethnic groups. The activities help pupils to interpret the graphs. Pupils are then asked to find and interpret information for their own local area.

## Further discussion suggestions

- New York is sometimes called a 'melting pot'. What does this mean?
- How multicultural is the UK?

## Answers to activities

**1 a and b**

|  | Newham | Chelsea |
|---|---|---|
| Closest to the city centre |  | ✓ |
| Has most people |  | ✓ |
| Has faster growth than London | ✓ | ✓ |
| Is most crowded |  | ✓ |
| Has most young people | ✓ |  |
| Has most at retirement age |  | ✓ |
| Has more over 40s than London |  | ✓ |
| Has fewest from Europe | ✓ |  |
| Has greatest mix of nationalities | ✓ |  |
| Likely to attract more migrants | ✓ |  |

**2 a** Allow a little leeway in terms of the percentages pupils attribute to different ethnic groups. However, percentages should add up to 100.

| | Ethnic groups | |
|---|---|---|
| | Newham | London |
| Highest (%) | 1 UK (34%) | 1 UK (61%) |
| | 2 Asia (32%) | 2 Others (12%) |
| | 3 Others (12%) | 3 Asia (9%) |
| | 4 Africa (12%) | 4 Europe (8%) |
| | 5 Caribbean (6%) | 5 Africa (5%) |
| Lowest (%) | 6 Europe (4%) | 6 Caribbean (5%) |

**b** The main difference between Newham and London as a whole is that Newham has a far greater percentage of the population from ethnic groups outside the UK. The largest ethnic group in both Newham and London are from the UK, but in London, the UK population is nearly double that of Newham. Newham has a larger percentage of population from Asia (32 per cent) – in London, less than 10 per cent of the population is from Asia.

**3 a–e**

The steps outlined in the pupil book were correct at the time of publication but bear in mind that websites can change. It would be best to check these steps are still valid before asking pupils to complete this activity. The pupil should be taken to a large selection of statistics for the chosen area including a small-scale map, census information, ethnicity and demographic data.

# 3 Population

**Pupil Book pages 66–67**

# The population enquiry

## About this spread

The population enquiry can either be used when pupils have completed the work on population distribution (pages 50–55), or at the end of the population unit. It is one of four enquiries in the pupil book and provides an opportunity to assess pupils' progress. Also look at the self-assessment checklist.

## What is the population enquiry about?

This enquiry builds on the work pupils have done earlier in this unit on where people live in the UK, what affects where people live (positive and negative factors) and the global distribution of population. The pupils' task is to decide on the most likely population distribution on an imaginary continent using positive and negative factors.

The enquiry should include:

- a copy of table B from page 66, which lists the negative and positive factors for the different areas on the continent, a decision on population density for each area along with the reasons for their decision
- a copy of map C from page 66, coloured to show the population distribution and the location of the main towns
- a description of the locations of the main towns, along with the reasons for their choice of locations.

## Learning objectives

On this spread pupils should learn:

- to interpret a map to identify positive and negative factors that affect population distribution.

## Learning outcomes

By the end of this spread pupils should be able to:

- complete a table of positive and negative factors, and population density for different areas
- draw a map showing population distribution
- give reasons for the location of towns on the map of population distribution.

## How can enquiries help with assessment?

For each enquiry in *Connections* there is a checklist in the appendices. The checklist provides pupils with success criteria so that they know what is expected in order to produce high-quality answers and improve in the future. The checklist can be used in two ways.

- Pupils can use these as they go along, to check that they are meeting the success criteria for the enquiry.
- They can be used for assessment either by you, as the teacher, or another pupil, for peer marking. Any element that is not ticked provides evidence that the pupil has not met all of the criteria.

## Differentiation suggestions

*For lower-ability pupils*

- Work with pupils to make sure they are clear about the steps they need to go through in order to complete the enquiry.
- Recap the work done through the chapter and particularly how positive and negative factors affect where people live.
- You could provide pupils with a copy of table B from page 66 that has been partially completed (e.g. for Areas 1 and 2), so that pupils understand how they should complete the table (see below).

- You could also provide pupils with a larger copy of map C so that they do not have to attempt to redraw it.

*For higher-ability pupils*

Ask pupils to describe the population distribution of a real country. You will need to provide them with maps showing the population distribution and the physical and human geography (e.g. in terms of industry, communications, resources, and so on). Pupils should refer to positive and negative factors in their answers.

| Area | Positive factors | Negative factors | Population density | Reasons |
|---|---|---|---|---|
| 1 | Mainly flat and low-lying | Poor thin soils<br>Little vegetation<br>Very cold | Few people | More negative than positive factors<br>Not good for farming<br>Nothing to support industry, so few jobs |
| 2 | Many lakes (water supply) | Hilly<br>Poor soils<br>Dense forest<br>Very cold winters | Few people | As for Area 1, more negative than positive factors<br>Not suitable for farming<br>Nothing to support industry<br>Very cold in winter |
| 3 | | | | |
| 4 | | | | |

## 4 India and Asia

**Pupil Book pages 70–71**

# What are Asia's main physical features?

### About this spread

Asia is the largest continent in the world and has a wide range of physical features including the highest mountains and some of the longest rivers. The aim of this spread is to introduce pupils to some of the contrasts from the wide, flat plains of the Ganges to the highest peaks in the Himalayas. The pupils are asked to use their map skills to familiarise themselves with the key physical features by looking at a relief map of the continent.

### Learning outcomes

By the end of this spread pupils should be able to:

- use a scale bar to measure distance
- use latitude and longitude to locate physical features
- write a description of physical features.

### Key vocabulary

- physical features

### Learning objectives

On this spread pupils should learn:

- the names of important physical features in Asia
- to understand the contrast between different areas of Asia.

### Skills builder

The use of longitude and latitude to pinpoint a place on the earth's surface is an important skill as it helps to locate a place precisely. It is a hard skill for pupils to learn as it does not start with zero in the bottom left corner. Zero degrees is found on the equator and also the Prime Meridian (Greenwich Meridian) and pupils need to be able to use N, E, S and W when referring to degrees of latitude and longitude to indicate the correct hemisphere that the place is located in.

### Further discussion suggestions

- What other physical features could be added to the map?
- Which tectonic plate is located here and which direction is it moving?

### Answers to activities

1. a  8,400 km (5,250 miles)

   b  10,760 km (6,725 miles)

   c  Because of the small scale it may be best to ask pupils to measure 'as the crow flies' from the source to the mouth of each river as shown on the map. As the crow flies answers will be something like the following:

   Yangtze 1,765 km (1,100 miles)

   Ganges 1,160 km (725 miles)

   Mekong 1,930 km (1,205 miles)

   d  2,500 km (1,560 miles)

2. Pupils' answers will vary.

   a  Lake Baikal 52 °N, 107 °E

   b  Mouth of the Ganges 22 °N, 92 °E

   c  Himalayas 30 °N, 80 °E

   d  Gobi Desert 45 °N, 100 °E

3. **Earthquakes and volcanic activity** Earthquakes and volcanoes occur on the plate boundaries in Asia. These follow the edge of the Pacific Ocean and is known as the 'Ring of Fire'. Some of the volcanoes in this area can be very explosive – the Krakatoa eruption of 1883 could be heard 4,800 km away. Large earthquakes have also caused devastating tsunamis such as in the Indian Ocean in 2004 and Japan in 2011.

**Vegetation features** Vegetation varies from very little in the Gobi Desert north of the Himalayas to ancient rainforest with a wide range of vegetation on the island of Borneo close to the equator.

**River features** The Himalayas create a lot of rain and this flows to the sea through some of the longest rivers in the world. The Ganges flows south through India into the Bay of Bengal, the Huang He and Yangtze flow east through China to the East China Sea and the Mekong flows along the border between Cambodia and Laos before it reaches the South China Sea.

4. Answers could be similar to the following,

   Photo A shows a flat area where rice is being grown in padi fields. There are a number of steep-sided rock formations sticking out of the landscape in the distance. There is one building showing a low population density in this area.

   Photo B shows Mount Everest, the highest mountain in the world. It is a snow-covered peak with a number of glaciers visible on its flanks. There are no people or buildings visible as is difficult to live there. Simply breathing is difficult as there is little oxygen in the atmosphere because of the altitude.

   Photo C shows a desert area in Jordan. The ground is sandy with a number of bare rock formations. The sky is clear and there are no clouds to reflect solar radiation. There are some tourists trekking through the desert using camels. There are no buildings in the photo as the lack of rainfall makes this a difficult place to live.

# 4 India and Asia

**Pupil Book pages 72–73**

## What are Asia's main human features?

### About this spread

Two out of every three people in the world live in Asia and it contains seven of the ten most populous cities. This shows the importance of understanding the main human features of the continent. In this spread pupils gain an understanding of where countries are and which countries they border. They also have an opportunity to look at why some areas of Asia have a high GDP and some of the resources available to trade and how this compares to some of the countries with a low GDP.

### Learning outcomes

By the end of this spread pupils should be able to:

- use latitude and longitude to locate places
- use a map to locate countries
- practise writing a description of human features.

### Key vocabulary

- human features
- labour
- malnutrition
- pollution
- exports
- natural resources

### Learning objectives

On this spread pupils should learn:

- to identify changes in population across Asia
- to understand the variation in wealth and growth
- to know the location of some countries in Asia.

### Skills builder

Using the map and the evidence boxes to help to write a description is a key skill for pupils to practise. The pupils are given the headings on which to base their descriptions and their first task is to scan the boxes surrounding the map for information. When the pupils have selected the information, they need to decide what point the evidence makes and why it is important. Writing in a specific structure of 'point–evidence–comment' will make it clear what the pupils are trying to describe.

### Further discussion suggestions

- How is China trying to control its population?
- What are the advantages and disadvantages of basing a call centre in India?

### Answers to activities

1. 
   a. Beijing 39°N, 115°E
   b. Tokyo 35°N, 140°E
   c. Bangkok 12°N, 101°E
   d. Delhi 27°N, 78°N
   e. Irkutsk 53°N, 105°E
   f. Singapore 1°N, 104°N

2. 
   a. India: Pakistan, China, Nepal, Bhutan, Bangladesh, Myanmar
   b. China: Mongolia, Russia, India, Myanmar, Kazakhstan, North Korea, Vietnam, Nepal, Pakistan, Bhutan, Laos, Afghanistan, Kyrgyzstan, Tajikistan (Note that Kyrgyzstan and Tajikistan are not named on the map on page 73.)
   c. Thailand: Myanmar, Laos, Cambodia, Malaysia

3. **Population** Asia is the most populous continent in the world with over 4.3 billion people which is 60 per cent of the world's population. China has the largest population with 1.4 billion people. There are 3,000 languages spoken with 600 spoken in Indonesia alone.

   **Industry and resources** There are a wide range of manufacturing industries in Asia due to the cheap labour. Fifteen per cent of the world's clothes are made in China which makes it the world's largest exporter. Asia has many natural resources such as oil. Half of the oil in the world comes from Saudi Arabia and other Middle East countries.

   **Growth and Wealth** There is a vast difference between the richest and poorest in Asia. The poorest countries, such as Nepal or Myanmar, have average earnings of about £620 a year. Other areas, such as China, are experiencing high levels of growth and have economies that are growing many times faster than the UK.

   **Problems** One problem that affects Asia is high levels of pollution. Seven of the world's most polluted cities are in China. Other issues include poverty, illiteracy, malnutrition and poor water supply.

4. Photo A shows a palace high on the hillside. It is a large building with many rooms, in contrast to the smaller one- or two-room buildings that are located at the bottom of the hill. In the foreground are people wearing brightly coloured clothing who appear to be looking after a group of small children.

   Photo B shows a city with a high population density. There are a number of multi-storey buildings some with more than ten floors. There is a road that appears to be suffering from congestion and the pavements are crowded with people.

   Photo C shows a modern skyline with a number of skyscrapers. One of the skyscrapers has an unusual construction with three spheres. In the foreground is an area of water that has a ship indicating that there may be a port.

# 4 India and Asia

**Pupil Book pages 74–75**

# India – a land of contrasts

## About this spread

India is a country that displays a vast contrast as it is large and populous, stretching from north of the Tropic of Cancer to close to the equator. There are contrasts in terms of landscape, climate, settlement and wealth. In this spread the pupils will have the opportunity to explore some of the contrasts that exist and describe the differing faces of the seventh largest country in the world.

## Learning objectives

On this spread pupils should learn:

- to understand the contrasts India displays
- the differences in relief, climate, vegetation, settlement and wealth.

## Learning outcomes

By the end of this spread pupils should be able to:

- describe the differences between different areas of India
- understand the key words associated with India
- use an atlas to find where places are.

## Key vocabulary

- monsoon
- chawls

## Skills builder

Photo interpretation is an important geographical skill for pupils to practise. Pupils can start to build up a picture of what an area is like by studying the relief, buildings and people that are in the photo. With an interpretation it is important that the pupils realise that they are making realistic suggestions about what the place is like and they are not going to know for certain. This will influence the language that they use in their answer.

## Further discussion suggestions

- Why do large contrasts in wealth occur in India?
- Why would people leave rural villages to move to larger cities?
- How does climate affect the food supply in different parts of India?

## Answers to activities

1. 
   a. The Ganges Valley is flat whereas the Himalayas are mountainous. The Ganges Valley is wet with padi fields in contrast to the Himalayas which are covered in snow and ice with no agriculture.
   
   b. North-west India is very dry and there is the Thar desert. The south of India is hot and wet enough for a rainforest to grow in Kerala.
   
   c. In the village scene in Kerala (photo D) there are few people whereas it is very busy in the city of Delhi (photo E). In Kerala you can see street-sellers in contrast to Delhi where you can see shops and stalls. In Kerala people are mainly wearing traditional dress whereas in Delhi they are wearing Western dress.
   
   d. In Uttar Pradesh you can see modern flats, constructed from concrete, set in parkland and with a swimming pool. This contrasts with the photo of slums in Kolkata. They are constructed from wood and material, have only one room and no facilities such as running water, electricity and sanitation.

2. The location of the following:
   
   a. Bustees, Kolkata
   
   b. The Taj Mahal, Agra
   
   c. Chawls, Mumbai
   
   d. Varanasi, Uttar Pradesh
   
   e. Tourist beaches, Goa
   
   f. A delta, River Ganges
   
   g. Tropical rainforest, Kerala
   
   h. A hot desert, Thar desert
   
   i. Kerala, Southern India
   
   j. Snow-covered mountains, Himalayas.

# 4 India and Asia

**Pupil Book pages 76–77**

## What are India's main physical features?

### About this spread

It is important for pupils to study the physical features of India because the country's traditional way of life is reliant on the heavy rains associated with the monsoon. Moisture-laden air, having crossed the Indian Ocean, is forced over the steep, rugged relief of the Himalayas, which leads to the creation of the south-west monsoon. On this page, pupils are asked to link the processes starting with plate tectonics and ending with heavy rainfall.

### Learning objectives

On this spread pupils should learn:

- about the variation in relief in India
- the causes of the monsoon and the effect is has on the people of India
- the advantages and disadvantages of the monsoon.

### Learning outcomes

By the end of this spread pupils should be able to:

- know how fold mountains, such as the Himalayas, are formed
- label diagrams to show how the monsoon occurs.

### Key vocabulary

- plate tectonics
- fold mountains
- earthquake
- monsoon
- relief rainfall

### Skills builder

This spread features a climate graph. Climate graphs have the potential to confuse pupils as they feature two sets of information on the same axes. The temperature is usually shown as a red line and the rainfall is usually shown as blue bars. This graph is drawn with one axis being shorter than the other, which helps pupils to avoid confusing the data. The other way for pupils to know if they have made an error is to see if their answer passes the 'common sense' test. If you read the graph and find that the temperature in December is 250 °C then this answer would fail that test.

### Further discussion suggestions

- Assess the usefulness of the monsoon for the people of India
- Why are temperature and rainfall displayed differently on a climate graph?
- What was the climate of India like before the Himalayas formed?

### Answers to activities

1. **a** The Indo-Australian plate is moving north and it has collided with the Eurasian plate. When the two plates meet they have crashed into each other and the rocks buckle forming the fold mountains of the Himalayas.

   **b** The Himalayas are still growing as the Indo-Australian plate is still moving north. If the plates get stuck then the pressure may be build up over many years. When the pressure is released the energy spreads out in a series of waves called earthquakes.

2. **a and b**

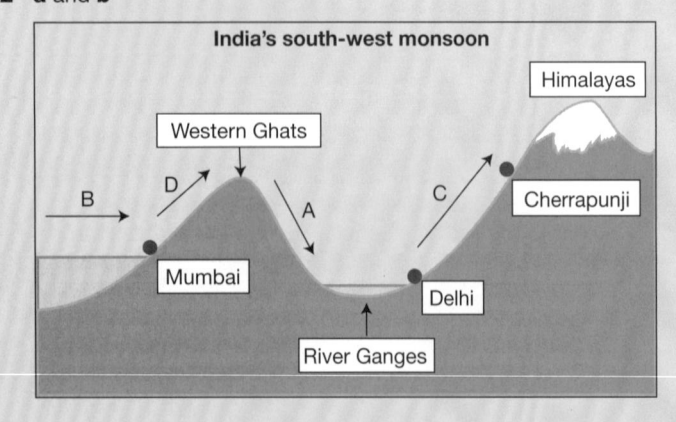

   India's south-west monsoon

   [Diagram with labels: Western Ghats, Himalayas, Mumbai, Delhi, Cherrapunji, River Ganges, with arrows B, D, A, C]

   **c** A Winds descend to give slightly drier conditions
   
   B Warm, moist winds blow across the Indian Ocean
   
   C Winds forced to rise again giving even heavier rain
   
   D Winds forced to rise, cool and give relief rainfall

3. **a** The south-west monsoon is important to India as it is needed to grow rice. The rain washes fertile soil onto the Ganges flood plain, as well as providing water for the padi fields.

   **b** If the monsoon provides too much rain then this can cause flooding, destroying people's houses and businesses. If there is too little rain then the rice crop may fail causing starvation.

## 4 India and Asia

**Pupil Book pages 78–79**

# What are India's main population features?

### About this spread

India's rapidly increasing population is the main feature of this spread. The population is not evenly spread in terms of density. Some areas are crowded and other areas are more sparsely populated. The population is not evenly balanced with a high percentage of young people under 19 and there is an even more pronounced effect if you consider the percentage of under 25 year olds. These patterns account for some of the issues that are facing India and provide an opportunity for pupils to gain an understanding of them.

### Learning outcomes

By the end of this spread pupils should be able to:

- read a population pyramid and draw conclusions
- be able to state some push and pull factors that cause rural-to-urban migration
- describe the problems that rural-to-urban migration can cause.

### Key vocabulary

- birth rate
- population pyramid
- life expectancy
- rural-to-urban migration

### Learning objectives

On this spread pupils should learn:

- that India has the world's second largest population
- population pyramids show that India has a young population
- rural-to-urban migration is occurring in India.

### Skills builder

Being able to interpret population pyramids is a skill that pupils can gain from the activities on this spread. A pyramid can be interpreted by dividing the pyramid into six sections, female children, male children, female adults, male adults, females over 65s and males over 65s. By examining the proportion of the six sections allows the pupil to draw conclusions about the population structure and the level of development displayed in the pyramid.

### Further discussion suggestions

- Should India introduce population policies such as China's one-child policy?
- How does India's population structure compare to the population structure of the United Kingdom?
- What might India's population pyramid look like in twenty years?

### Answers to activities

1. **a**
   **i** 1950
   India, 0.35 billion
   China, 0.58 billion
   
   **ii** 2010
   India, 1.1 billion
   China, 1.31 billion
   
   **b** Since the 1990s, India has had a faster growing population than China. This is because India has a high birth rate and people are starting to live longer despite having a low life expectancy (69 years old). China's population is not growing as fast as they operate a one-child policy that limits the birth rate.
   
   **c** The populations of India and China are estimated to be equal in 2028.

2. **a**
   **i** Under 15, 31.7%
   **ii** Over 65, 5.1%
   
   **b** An advantage of a large percentage of young people is a large potential workforce.
   
   A disadvantage of a large percentage of young people is that more money is needed to provide schools and education.
   
   An advantage of a small percentage of older people is that not much money is required for state pensions or medical facilities.
   
   A disadvantage of a small percentage of older people means the loss of support networks – for instance, child minding.

3. The correct statements are:
   - India's population is not evenly spread.
   - Most people live along the Ganges valley.
   - Fewest people live in the north-west desert.
   - India has the three of the world's largest cities.

4. **a** Reasons to leave the countryside might include drought, famine, unemployment or lack of education. They are push factors.
   
   Reasons to move to the city might include the prospect of jobs, food supply, education, medical facilities or food supply. They are pull factors.
   
   **b** This process is called rural-to-urban migration.

5. The problems of India's increasing population include:
   - Not enough space or resources for people to use. This means that they have to live close together in poorly constructed houses that lack facilities such as sanitation or electricity.
   - There are not enough jobs, so people do not have money for education or health care.
   - The transport system may become overloaded and lead to congestion and air pollution.

# 4 India and Asia

**Pupil Book pages 80–81**

# What is it like living in Mumbai?

## About this spread

This spread looks at the housing in Mumbai and highlights the wide contrasts in living standards that can be seen in the city. In the 'Gateway to India' area of the city, the pupils will study the wealthier areas of the city with Bollywood stars amongst the people who live and work there. The pupils will be able to contrast this area with the lower-quality chawls and the slum residences that are found in Dharavi. The images help pupils to build up an idea of what each area looks like and asks them to consider what the standard of living in each area will be like.

## Learning outcomes

By the end of this spread pupils should be able to:
- describe the location of wealthy housing in Mumbai
- list the advantages and disadvantages of chawls
- know the characteristics of Mumbai's shanty settlements.

## Key vocabulary

- shanty settlement
- chawl
- sewage

## Learning objectives

On this spread pupils should learn:
- that Mumbai is a city of contrasts with both rich and poor areas
- wealthier areas of Mumbai are located centrally
- shanty settlements are built on marginal land.

## Skills builder

Describing the location of different types of housing using the map for evidence is an important geographical skill. Every sentence that the pupil writes needs to contain at least one of the 4 'Ds' (data, distance, direction and density). On this spread, data represents the best quality houses. The scale bar can be used to calculate distance and the compass rose provides pupils with direction. High-quality descriptive sentences would try and contain all three of these elements.

## Further discussion suggestions

- Can the pupils find indicators such as life expectancy to contrast the two areas of Mumbai?
- Why are the wealthy areas of housing all located on the coast?
- What is a day in the life of a resident in Dharavi like?

## Answers to activities

1. **a** There are a number of different areas of best-quality houses. There is a 6 km stretch on the shore of the Arabian Sea around 10 km to the north of the CBD. A second area of high-quality houses lies to the west of the CBD. It is a 4 km area on the shore of the Arabian Sea that is linked to the CBD. A further area of high-quality housing is 2 km south of the CBD at the end of the peninsula overlooking the Arabian Gulf.
   **b** Bollywood stars live here as they are close to the cinema industry. They have large, well-built houses with ocean views connected by wide roads and plenty of services such as shops and nightclubs.
2. **a** A chawl is a four- or five-storey building that consists of a long corridor connecting up to 20 dwellings that are generally two rooms with a balcony. One room is for living and sleeping, the other is for cooking and eating. They also have a balcony overlooking the street. They often have a shared toilet block. Electricity connections are common.
   **b** Good points: reasonable construction; electricity connection; more than one room; good community spirit.
   **c** Bad points: overcrowded; shared toilet facilities; noisy.
3. **a** A shanty town is a collection of poor-quality housing made from materials such as wood, mud or cardboard. They are often in marginal areas and have no facilities.
   **b** Four problems could include: poorly constructing buildings; lack of sanitation; high population density; no electricity connection.
   **c** People living in the shanty towns have jobs recycling materials such as plastic, tin cans and old drums.

## 4 India and Asia

**Pupil Book pages 82–83**

# What is it like living in a village in India?

## About this spread

Around half the population of Kerala lives in traditional villages where subsistence farming is the main way of life. Pupils will study how the residents of villages in Kerala live and work. The pupils will investigate the types of crops that are grown and how valuable the cow is to the villages for ploughing the land and for fertilizer. The role of non-governmental organisations, such as WaterAid, in providing clean water to the residents of the villages is also studied by the pupils.

## Learning objectives

On this spread pupils should learn:

- about the traditional method of life in an Indian village
- the method of farming in an Indian village
- how WaterAid is helping to improve the standard of living.

## Learning outcomes

By the end of this spread pupils should be able to:

- describe conditions in a traditional Indian village
- compare and contrast a traditional Indian village with a UK village.

## Skills builder

The activities on this spread test the skill of contrasting two areas. Pupils can increase the complexity of their work by dividing it up into a series of ideas such as building materials or farming methods. Filling in the table in detail allows the pupils to analyse where the biggest differences are. The pupils could then rank them in order of the most important differences between the two villages. This would then be the starting point for the pupils to write a paragraph to summarise their comparison.

## Further discussion suggestions

- What role do other non-governmental organisations (NGOs) have in India?
- What problems can burning dung cause?

## Answers to activities

1. Kerala is in the **south** of India. It has a **monsoon** climate with **high** temperatures all year and a very **wet** summer. It is mainly a **rural** area and the state is relatively **wealthy**.

2. 

|  | Village in Kerala | Village in your local area |
|---|---|---|
| Road | There is one road. It is dusty in the dry season and flooded in the monsoon season. | Tarmac minor road linking it to 'A' roads. |
| Transport | Cars, cyclists, handcarts and trishaws make the road busy. | Most people have their own car. There is a bus service. |
| Building materials | Buildings are made from mud bricks with palm fronds used for the roof. | Buildings are made from brick and concrete. They have tiles and slate roofs. |
| Shops | There are a few shops and market stalls selling local grown food. | There are a number of small shops like a post office and general store. |
| Fruit/vegetables | Bananas, ginger, tapioca and other vegetables are grown. | People buy a wide range of fruit and vegetables from the shops. |
| Farming methods | Farming is done by hand with the use of a cow for some jobs such as ploughing. | Farming is highly mechanised using tractors and combine harvesters. |
| Crops/animals | The main crop is rice but they also grow other crops such as bananas. The cow is the most valuable animal. | Farms grow a range of crops such as wheat and barley and keep herds of animals like cows or sheep. |
| Water supply | Water Aid has provided a pump so the villagers don't have to walk to the river to get water. | Everyone has a connection to running water. |
| Sewage | The river is used to dispose of sewage. | Everyone has a connection to sanitation. |
| Fuel | Wood, palm fronds, crop waste and animal dung are used for fuel. | People have electricity and gas connected to their house. They can buy petrol or diesel for their cars. |

## 4 India and Asia

**Pupil Book pages 84–85**

# How interdependent is India?

### About this spread

The growth of trade in India with its Asian neighbours is the main topic of this spread. Pupils have the opportunity to study how India currently exports low value items such as foodstuffs, minerals and timber whilst importing higher value items such as cars, machinery and electrical goods. Pupils will see how India is increasingly trading with other Asian countries at the expense of other continents, especially North America and Europe.

### Learning outcomes

By the end of this spread pupils should be able to:

- define key words linked to interdependence
- explain why some countries have trade surplus and others have a trade deficit
- analyse a diagram to determine changes in Indian trade in the last 20 years.

### Key vocabulary

- interdependent
- trade
- exports
- imports
- trade balance
- trade surplus
- trade deficit

### Learning objectives

On this spread pupils should learn:

- the key terms surrounding international trade
- the reasons why developing countries have a trade deficit
- that India is becoming increasingly interdependent.

### Skills builder

One of the activities that this spread asks pupils to compete is to analyse a diagram and use it to suggest what may happen in the future. There are no axes on the diagram so pupils will have to look at the pattern of the changes and decide:

- which areas of the world are increasing their direction of trade with India
- which areas of the world are decreasing their direction of trade with India.

After the pupils have decided what the changes in future will be, they can use the bars on the diagram to decide on the rate of change.

### Further discussion suggestions

- How does India's balance of trade compare to other countries in the world?
- Which companies are based in India and what products do they import or export?

### Answers to activities

**1 a** An interdependent country is one that works with other countries to provide skills, resources or technology.

**b** India has to import goods such as crude oil, gold and silver and electrical goods from other countries.

**2 Trade** The movement and sale of goods between countries.

**Imports** Goods brought by a country that were produced in other countries.

**Exports** Goods and services produced in one country that are sold to other countries.

**Trade surplus** When a country earns more from its exports than it spends on imports.

**Trade deficit** When a country spends more money on its imports than it earns from its exports.

**3 a** Developed countries tend to have a trade surplus as they import cheap raw materials, turn them into something more valuable and then export a more valuable product. An example is importing steel to make cars which are then exported.

**b** Some developing countries have a trade deficit because they export the cheap raw material (such as copper) and import the more expensive manufactured product (electrical items).

**4 a** Diagram E shows that India has increased its trade with other areas of Asia but decreased the amount that it trades with Europe, North America, Africa and Latin America.

**b** In the future India will become more developed so there will be more demand for oil which it will need to import from the Middle East. It will also need to import more manufactured goods from China.

# 4 India and Asia

**Pupil Book pages 86–87**

# The India enquiry

## About this spread

The population enquiry can either be used when pupils have completed the work on the India unit or after they have some knowledge of development indicators. It asks pupils to consider a lot of data and select the information that they consider to be of the most use. It is one of four enquiries in the pupil book, and provides an opportunity to assess pupils' progress.

## Learning objectives

On this spread pupils should learn:

- to select information that demonstrates the levels of development in India.

## Learning outcomes

By the end of this spread pupils should be able to:

- know different ways that development in India can be measured
- draw bar graphs
- justify a decision using evidence.

## Key vocabulary

- development
- GNP (gross national product)

## What is the India enquiry about?

This enquiry builds on the work pupils have done earlier in this unit on economic factors of India and Asia and tries to place India in the world based on different development indicators. The pupils' task is to decide on the best development indicators and to consider whether India is developing. They also need to consider where India's fast growing economy might lead in future.

The enquiry should include:

- definitions and explanations of the key words from the topic
- a copy of diagram B from page 66 of the pupil book, which lays out the pupil's opinion on which is the best development indicator
- a conclusion summing up India's current level of development and what may happen in future.

## How can enquiries help with assessment?

For each enquiry in *Connections* there is a checklist in the appendices. The checklist provides pupils with success criteria so that they know what is expected in order to produce high-quality answers and improve in the future. The checklist can be used in two ways.

- Pupils can use them as they go along, to check that they are meeting the success criteria for the enquiry.
- They can be used for assessment either by you, as the teacher, or another pupil, for peer marking. Any element that is not ticked provides evidence that the pupil has not met all of the criteria.

## Differentiation suggestions

*For lower-ability pupils*

- Work with pupils to make sure they are clear about the steps they need to go through in order to complete the enquiry.
- Recap the work done in chapter 4 of the pupil book, particularly what development is and how it can be measured.
- Work with the pupils to determine and draw the axes for each graph or provide a diamond outline for the pupils to fill in.
- You could also provide pupils with headings.

*For higher-ability pupils*

There are a couple of possibilities.

Ask pupils to describe the population distribution of a real country. You will need to provide them with maps showing the population distribution and the physical and human geography (e.g. in terms of industry, communications, resources, and so on). Pupils should refer to positive and negative factors in their answers.

These pupils should be required to give their reasons for the conclusions they reach. Instead of merely drawing the bar graphs they should be required to describe and interpret them, and indicate any similarities and differences. Any exceptions to the general picture that emerges should be noted.

Opportunities could be given for these pupils to research other measures of development that may, or may not support the conclusions reached based on the measures covered on the spread. For example, percentage of population with access to safe water, number of tractors per 1000 population. They could also be introduced to the Human Development Index (HDI) which, instead of using a single measure, combines literacy rate, life expectancy and infant mortality to give an indication of the population's quality of life rather than by just measuring their standard of living.

## 5 World issues

**Pupil Book pages 90–91**

# What is climate change?

### About this spread

This spread is the first in the unit on world issues. This unit looks at some of the major problems facing our world, including climate change, energy use, the problems of food supply and water shortages, and the issue of poverty. The term 'global warming' describes the way our planet is heating up. It is a world problem to which we all contribute – but some more than others. This spread explains that climate change is thought to be the result of the greenhouse effect, and how the burning of fossil fuels acts to increase the greenhouse effect, meaning the earth becomes warmer.

### Learning outcomes

By the end of this spread pupils should be able to:

- understand that burning fossil fuels has caused an increase in temperatures around the world – this is global warming
- explain the greenhouse effect
- give reasons why climate change is a world problem
- explain why international agreement is needed to reduce greenhouse gases
- understand that global warming is a cause of climate change.

### Key vocabulary

- ice age
- climate change
- global warming
- greenhouse effect

### Learning objectives

On this spread pupils should learn:

- that global warming is the heating up of the earth
- what the greenhouse effect is
- that global warming is a cause of climate change.

### Skills builder

Pupils need to be able to use and interpret a wide range of graphs and diagrams in geography. On this spread, pupils need to be able to understand two different types of graphs – a line graph (A) that shows the increases in both temperature and carbon dioxide emissions since 1860, and a pie graph (D) that shows the percentages of different greenhouse gases. Pupils are asked to describe what graph A shows and explain the link between the changes in global temperatures and carbon dioxide levels.

Diagrams B and C in the pupil book show what the greenhouse effect is and also what causes it. Pupils use diagram C to draw their own diagram to explain how burning fossil fuels may cause global warming.

### Further discussion suggestions

- Could global warming be linked to natural changes rather than human activity?
- Could a gigantic volcanic eruption (which would release greenhouse gases) undo efforts to reduce greenhouse gas emissions?

### Answers to activities

1. **a** Global temperatures have risen by 1 °C (from 13.4 °C to 14.4 °C) from 1860 to 2000. Although the overall trend has been upwards, there has not been a continuous rise in temperature. Temperatures have fallen back, e.g. around 1910, 1950 and 1970. Since 1970, there has been a further increase in temperature.
   
   **b** Carbon dioxide levels have increased throughout the period shown on the graph. There has been a faster increase in carbon dioxide levels since 1940.
   
   **c** As carbon dioxide levels have increased, so have average global temperatures.

2. **a** Climate change is the long-term change in the earth's climate which can be reflected in either an increase or a decrease in average temperatures.
   
   **b** Global warming is the heating up of the planet.
   
   **c** The gases that surround the earth act like a greenhouse, trapping some of the sun's heat and warming the earth. This is known as the greenhouse effect.
   
   **d** Global warming can be described as a world problem because almost all of the world's countries contribute to the problem by producing greenhouse gases. It also affects every country in the world.

3. **a and b**
   
   1 Sun's heat passes through greenhouse gases
   2 Earth is warmed up
   3 Burning fossil fuels causes an increase in greenhouse gases
   4 Increased amount of greenhouse gases means less heat escapes into space
   5 More heat is trapped, warming the Earth further

4. **a** Carbon dioxide and nitrous oxide result from burning coal, oil and natural gas.
   
   **b** International agreement is needed to reduce greenhouse gases because nearly all countries contribute to the production of greenhouse gases, and all countries are affected by global warming.
   
   **c** Pupils' lists will vary, but they should be thinking about how they travel, how their homes are heated, the food they eat and the products they use.

# 5 World issues

**Pupil Book pages 92–93**

# What are the effects of climate change?

## About this spread

This spread follows on from pages 90–91 of the pupil book and looks at the effects of global warming and climate change. No one can say exactly what the effects will be, but scientists have made many predictions. Some of the effects are already being felt. This spread looks at the likely effects climate change will have, both on the world as a whole and on the UK.

## Learning objectives

On this spread pupils should learn:

- about the possible effects of climate change on both the world and the UK.

## Learning outcomes

By the end of this spread pupils should be able to:

- describe how climate change will cause problems around the world because of rising sea levels and more extreme variations in weather.
- describe how some of the effects may bring benefits to the UK, while others will cause problems.

## Skills builder

The work on pages 90–91 and this spread should enable pupils to make the link between how human activity, including their own, affects the environment. Many of our activities involve burning fossil fuels, which produce greenhouse gases that contribute to global warming. The activities in the pupil book and those suggested here should help pupils to understand that we all contribute to climate change and can all do something about it. These spreads also help pupils to understand the problem at different scales – a personal scale, national scale and global scale.

## Further discussion suggestions

- We are due another Ice Age – is climate change preventing it from happening?
- Should low-lying countries such as the Netherlands and Bangladesh be urgently considering constructing coastal flood barriers?
- What might be the effect of climate change on tundra permafrost, which stores large amounts of carbon and methane?

## Answers to activities

1. ①= Arctic Ocean
   ②= Great Plains
   ③= Caribbean Sea
   ④= London (UK)
   ⑤= Amazon
   ⑥= Sahara Desert
   ⑦= Mediterranean Sea
   ⑧= Alps
   ⑨= Maldives
   ⑩= Bangladesh
   ⑪= Europe

2. **a, b** and **c**

   Flow chart:
   - Temperature rises →
     - Ice cap melts → Sea levels rise
     - Water expands → Sea levels rise
     - Climate changes → Plants and wildlife affected

   **Sea levels rise – Effects include:**
   - Many major cities flooded
   - Increased flooding in coastal regions
   - Islands submerged by rising sea levels
   - Beaches disappear as sea levels rise

   **Plants and wildlife affected – Effects include:**
   - Drier conditions reduce grain harvest
   - Drier conditions cause loss of rainforest
   - Desert advances north to replace crops
   - Places with less rain may experience food shortages as crops fail to grow
   - Plants and animals that cannot adapt to climate change will become extinct
   - There might be an increase in insect pests

3. **a** In the UK, the area for growing cereal crops will increase, and mediterranean-type summers in the south of England means that farmers will be able to grow maize, vines, oranges and peaches.

   **b** The greatest problems will include: there will be more pests and diseases because of milder winters; coastal ports and low-lying areas will be flooded; there will be a greater risk of forest fires.

   **c** Pupils' responses will depend on where they live.

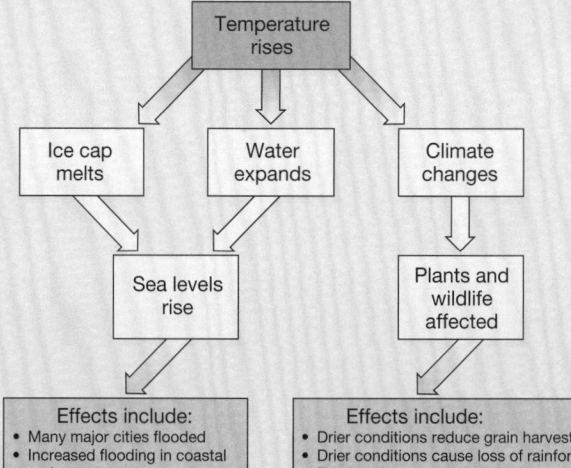

# 5 World issues

## Pupil Book pages 94–95
## How can our energy use change?

### About this spread

This spread considers our energy use today, which depends heavily on fossil fuels, and how that might change in the future. The type and source of our energy supplies will have to change because fossil fuels are a finite resource and current known supplies of oil and gas are likely to run out within pupils' lifetimes. Pupils consider the changes in our energy use 15 years from now and 50 years from now.

### Learning objectives

On this spread pupils should learn:

- that energy use will have to change in the future
- that some experts believe that in the future, wind, solar and hydrogen power will meet most of the world's energy needs.

### Learning outcomes

By the end of this spread pupils should be able to:

- describe how energy use is likely to change in the future
- explain the impact of the changes in energy use.

### Key vocabulary

- fossil fuels

### Skills builder

Making accurate predictions is a skill that pupils can practise in this spread. By looking at the diagrams pupils can see how energy use is changing. The first step is to look at each energy type individually in each of the diagrams to see how they change over time. From there you can identify if there is a trend and suggest how this trend may change in future.

### Further discussion suggestions

- Why is nuclear power unpopular?
- What happened at the Fukushima nuclear power plant?
- What are the advantages and disadvantages of different types of renewable energy?

### Answers to activities

1. **a** Oil is the energy resource that is most used today. It provides 41 per cent of the world's energy needs and is used to generate electricity, heat homes and power aircraft, cars and other vehicles.

   **b** Hydrogen is likely to be the most used energy resource in 50 years' time. It is likely to replace oil for heating homes, to power cars, buses and planes, and to generate electricity.

2. **a** Nuclear power and natural gas are likely to be used less. (Oil and coal are unlikely to be used at all.)

   **b** Solar and wind power are likely to be used more. (Hydrogen is likely to be a main energy source.)

3. Fossil fuels contribute to global warming because they produce greenhouse gases when they are burned. As their use declines, the increase in global warming should also be reduced. New sources of energy such as hydrogen, along with wind and solar power, are 'clean' sources that do not produce greenhouse gases, and so will not lead to an increase in global warming.

4. Pupils' responses will vary, but they should mention activities they do that currently rely on the use of oil.

5. Pupils' responses will vary, but they should mention that the energy sources we will be using in 50 years' time are likely to be renewable and clean, so they will not contribute to climate change.

# 5 World issues

**Pupil Book pages 96–97**

# What is the water problem?

## About this spread

This spread considers the fact that many people around the world do not have access to a safe, clean, reliable supply of water. It looks at the causes and effects of the water supply problem in developing countries which is likely to get worse rather than better. The UN predicts that the number of people short of fresh water will rise which could lead to conflict between countries that share the same water supply.

## Learning outcomes

By the end of this spread pupils should be able to:

- understand that many people have no reliable supply of clean water
- describe the link between the country's wealth and access to clean water
- describe how organisations and individuals can help in providing clean water for people in developing countries.

## Learning objectives

On this spread pupils should learn:

- about the reasons for water shortages in developing countries
- about the effects of water shortages in developing countries
- how voluntary organisations can help to improve the water supply problem.

## Skills builder

Pupils should be in no doubt that the lack of clean water is a major world issue and that, as demand for water grows, so the pressure on this resource increases. The way this spread is structured allows pupils to see some of the causes of the water supply problem, and the effects this problem has. The ability to identify causes and effects is a useful skill that is reinforced in the activities.

## Further discussion suggestions

- Why does the Colorado river dry up before it reaches its estuary?
- The south and east of Britain are more prone to droughts than the wetter, more mountainous north and west. Could water be transported to the south and east from north-west reservoirs via a network of pipes and rivers?
- How can taking ground water from aquifers possibly damage buildings above?

## Answers to activities

1. **a** Many people are short of water because: as more people move to cities (rural-to-urban migration) more water is needed; wells can dry up as more water is used; lack of rain can cause drought.

    **b** Developing countries have neither the money nor the technology to create reservoirs or lay water pipes; many towns and cities have their limited water supplies polluted as a result of poor sewerage and hygiene.

2. **a** Over 3 billion people are likely to be short of clean, reliable water by 2050.

    **b** Many of the world's largest 250 rivers flow through more than one country. This may cause problems in providing water for people where countries want to protect their own supply of water. In future, rivers may become polluted or dry up (if, for example, too much water is extracted or there is less rainfall).

3. **a** 
    - Countries in order of wealth are (wealthiest first): USA, UK, China, Brazil, Kenya, Bangladesh.
    - Countries in order of access to clean water (highest percentage first): USA and UK, China and Bangladesh, Brazil, Kenya.

    **b** Wealthier countries generally have better access to a safe water supply than poorer countries. Wealthier countries can afford to create reservoirs and lay pipes to provide a good supply of clean water to more of the population than poorer developing countries can.

4. **a** Organisations like WaterAid collect money through donations. This is used to provide clean water, for example through taps and wells, and improve sanitation in developing countries.

    **b** Pupils' responses will vary depending on their own point of view.

# 5 World issues

**Pupil Book pages 98–99**

# Food – too little or too much?

## About this spread

This spread looks at the issue of food. According to the UN, there is enough food for the world's population, but while some parts of the world eat too much (or the wrong type of food) other parts of the world go hungry. Furthermore, this problem is likely to get worse. By 2050, around half the world's population is likely to be underfed and suffering from malnutrition. This spread makes the point that the main cause of malnutrition is not a lack of food availability, but is caused by poverty – people cannot afford to buy food.

## Learning outcomes

By the end of this spread pupils should be able to:

- understand that there are considerable differences in the quantity and quality of food supplies between rich and poor countries
- classify the causes of food shortages in poor countries
- describe the causes and effects of malnutrition and obesity.

## Key vocabulary

- diet
- obese
- malnutrition

## Learning objectives

On this spread pupils should learn:

- about why people in some parts of the world are short of food
- about the effects of eating too little, or too much, food.

## Skills builder

Activity 1 asks pupils to list the causes of food shortages under different headings. This is a straightforward sorting or classification exercise. Classification is a skill that pupils will need to use in other instances in geography, whether it is classifying jobs by type of industry (primary, secondary, tertiary) or resources as renewable, non-renewable, and so on.

In Activity 3, pupils are asked to rank countries (i.e. put them in order) according to the percentage of people suffering from obesity and malnutrition. Again, ranking is a skill that pupils will find useful, not only in geography, but in other subjects as well.

## Further discussion suggestions

- The world produces enough food to feed every one of its 7 billion inhabitants, but the food is often in the wrong place, is unaffordable or cannot be stored long enough. How can the problem of feeding the world's hungry people be solved?
- More than 80 per cent of rural Africans are smallholders farming less than an acre of land. How can they be given tools and training to produce more food?
- Should we look to politicians, rather than charities, to 'feed the world'?

## Answers to activities

1. **Natural causes** Drought – places that rely on rain for crops and grass for animals may have none for several years; insects such as locusts can eat the crop.

   **Caused by rich countries** Poor countries often have to rely on food from other countries, which is expensive to buy; global warming is predicted to reduce the amount of crops.

   **Caused by poor countries** Corruption – people in authority keep food and aid for themselves and do not share it with those who need it; poorer countries have large populations that need feeding; civil war ruins crops and kills farm animals.

2. a  Pupils should describe what would be a good diet for themselves. The average number of calories consumed by people living in rich countries is around 3,400, but the average for the UK is approximately 3,800. The number of calories needed is below 3,400. Pupils should indicate the type of food that would give them a healthy diet. They should mention the quality of food and the mix of protein, carbohydrates and vitamins, etc.

   b  Pupils should suggest changes to their present diet to help themselves and their family live a healthier life.

3. a

|   | % obese | % malnourished |
|---|---|---|
| 1 | USA | Bangladesh |
| 2 | UK | Kenya |
| 3 | Brazil | China |
| 4 | Kenya | Brazil |
| 5 | China, Bangladesh | UK, USA |

   b  'Obesity' is the term used for someone who is overweight.

   c  Obesity is caused by eating too much of the wrong kinds of foods. The effects of obesity include heart problems and breathing difficulties.

   d  'Malnutrition' is ill-health caused by a shortage of food or a poor diet.

   e  Malnutrition is usually caused by the fact that people do not have enough money to buy food, rather than the fact that food is not available. Malnutrition causes diseases such as kwashiorkor, marasmus and rickets.

# 5 World issues

**Pupil Book pages 100–101**

# What is the poverty problem?

## About this spread

This spread considers the issue of poverty. Around the world, there are approximately 1 billion people living in extreme poverty on less than $1.25 a day – a tiny amount of money. People living in poor countries are often trapped in a cycle of poverty. This spread looks at the daily life of one woman, Marietta, as she struggles to survive in south-east Kenya.

## Learning outcomes

By the end of this spread pupils should be able to:
- describe what is meant by 'the cycle of poverty'
- describe how one person is caught in the cycle of poverty
- describe the problems caused by poverty in poor countries.

## Key vocabulary

- extreme poverty
- cycle of poverty

## Learning objectives

On this spread pupils should learn:
- about the cycle of poverty
- about some of the causes and effects of poverty.

## Skills builder

This spread and, in particular, Marietta's story on page 100 of the pupil book will encourage pupils to understand how other people's lives differ drastically from their own. Marietta's story will open their eyes to the fact that millions of people all over the world live on very little – their quality of life and standard of living are worlds away from those that many of us take for granted in the UK. Marietta's story will encourage pupils to empathise with someone else from a different culture. It will help them to appreciate that other people hold values and attitudes that are very different from their own.

## Further discussion suggestions

- What is the World Bank and how does it help the world's poorer countries?
- Why are most of the countries in Africa plagued by poverty when Africa is so rich in natural resources such as oil, diamonds, gold, silver, iron, bauxite and copper?

## Answers to activities

1 a 'The cycle of poverty' is when the level of poverty gets worse year after year, with little hope of improvement.

b

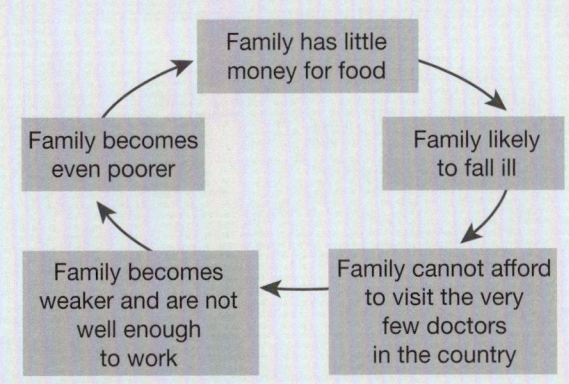

```
Family has little money for food
    ↓
Family likely to fall ill
    ↓
Family cannot afford to visit the very few doctors in the country
    ↓
Family becomes weaker and are not well enough to work
    ↓
Family becomes even poorer
    ↑ (back to top)
```

c Marietta is responsible for her seven young children. The eldest children go to school, but have to collect water first and then walk to school.

Marietta does not work outside the home as she has no time and so cannot earn any extra money. She would not have the money to pay any extra bills if, for example, the animals needed a vet.

d Pupils' responses will vary, but in essence their lives will be different from Marietta's in many respects such as housing, health care, education, jobs, food, and so on.

2 a The two poorest countries are Bangladesh and Kenya.

b The problems caused by poverty include: lack of jobs; poor quality housing; problems with trade; lack of transport; food may be poor in quality or insufficient in quantity; lack of schools and shortage of hospitals and medical care; not enough resources.

c Pupils are asked to describe five of the problems caused by poverty in poor countries. Answers could include:
- a lack of jobs means little or no income
- poor quality housing may lack electricity, clean water or sewage disposal
- country may have few exports, so they earn little money to buy the goods they lack
- a lack of transport makes the movement of people and goods difficult
- people become weak when not enough food is grown to provide a good diet
- a lack of schools means people are poorly educated and a shortage of hospitals and medical care means people are in poor health
- there may be too many people for the resources available.

# 5 World issues

**Pupil Book pages 102–103**

# How might poverty be reduced?

## About this spread

This spread follows on from pages 100–101 and addresses the issue of how poverty in poorer countries might be reduced. In order to improve their lives, people in poorer countries need to break free from the cycle of poverty. This spread looks at different ways this might be achieved – through aid, reducing debt and self-help approaches.

## Learning outcomes

By the end of this spread pupils should be able to:

- describe the differences between short-term and long-term aid
- give some advantages and disadvantages of short-term and long-term aid
- describe how charities such as Practical Action can help to reduce poverty through self-help schemes.

## Key vocabulary

- short-term aid
- long-term aid
- debt

## Learning objectives

On this spread pupils should learn:

- how poverty in poor countries can be reduced by giving aid, reducing debt and through self-help schemes.

## Skills builder

This spread asks pupils to write a description of how Practical Action has helped Marietta, using specific headings. To help pupils develop this skill there are a number of steps that can be taken. The first step is to collect key words that will structure the description. This can either be completed by highlighting key words on a photocopy of the page or by producing a mind map for each heading. Pupils can then add other adjectives that are relevant to their description to increase its complexity. Each point can then be numbered with '1' being the first sentence of their paragraph.

## Further discussion activities

- Should all the world's poor countries have their debt cancelled?
- Are consumers willing to pay more for things like fair trade products to help people in poorer countries?

## Answers to activities

1. **a** 'Aid' is the giving of resources such as money, medical equipment, food supplies or human helpers to another country.

   **b** Short-term aid is often given to a country after a natural disaster such as an earthquake, flood or tsunami. Long-term aid is often money borrowed from richer countries or organisations such as the World Bank.

   **c** *Short-term aid*
   - Advantages include: provides help exactly when needed; provides targeted help (such as food, medical equipment following a natural disaster).
   - Disadvantages include: aid is provided for a limited period of time; it does not help to reduce overall poverty.

   *Long-term aid*
   - Advantages include: countries borrow money, which means they can afford to buy goods and services from other countries; it provides long-term help, which could help countries develop.
   - Disadvantages include: interest has to be paid on loans, so poor countries fall further into debt as they have to keep on borrowing to pay off debts; it widens the gap between rich and poor countries.

2. **a and b**

   - Help people over a long period of time
   - Encourage people to help themselves
   - Improve building materials, e.g. roof tiles and bricks
   - Develop sustainable energy suitable for use in local situation
   - Educate people so they can improve their own lives
   - Develop improved cooking stoves to use less firewood (and so reduce the amount of time needed to collect wood)
   - Teach people to become independent

   **c**
   - Training/education: Marietta was given a five-day course to recognise and treat livestock diseases, and learn basic animal care.
   - Benefits to herself: She earns money from the sale of vaccines and medicine, which means she can buy food when it is needed, and she can keep her own cows healthy.
   - Benefits to others: Others can bring animals to her surgery, or she can visit them at home to treat diseases, give vaccines and keep animals healthy.

# 5 World issues

**Pupil Book pages 104–105**

# The world issues enquiry

## About this spread

The world issues enquiry is intended to be used at the end of the world issues unit. It is one of four enquiries in the pupil book, and provides an opportunity to assess pupils' progress.

## Learning outcomes

By the end of this spread pupils should be able to:

- use different sources of information to look at the effect of the coffee trade, and the change to fair trade on coffee growers and consumers
- write a report on fair trade.

## Key vocabulary

- fair trade

## How can enquiries help assessment?

For each enquiry in *Connections* there is a checklist in the appendices. The checklist provides pupils with success criteria so that they know what is expected in order to produce high-quality answers and improve in the future. The checklist can be used in two ways.

- Pupils can use these as they go along, to check that they are meeting the success criteria for the enquiry.
- They can be used for assessment either by you, as the teacher, or another pupil, for peer marking. Any element that is not ticked provides evidence that the pupil has not met all of the criteria.

## Learning objectives

On this spread pupils should learn:

- about how trade works and the impact it has on people in poorer countries
- about how fair trade can help to reduce poverty in poorer countries.

## What is the world issues enquiry about?

In this enquiry, pupils find out what trade is and how poorer countries tend not to get a fair deal when it comes to trade. They learn that the trade issue is one of the reasons why poor countries stay poor and people live in poverty. Fair trade is one of the ways that can help people make more money from trade and therefore lift people out of poverty. In this enquiry, the pupils' task is to explain the main points of fair trade to a company called Kenya Coffee and suggest how it can become a fair trade company.

In the enquiry, pupils:

- find out where the money goes when coffee is sold
- think about the impacts of fair trade on poverty, the growers, the environment and people in the UK
- write a report for Kenya Coffee on fair trade.

## Differentiation suggestions

### For lower-ability pupils

Work with pupils to make sure they are clear about the steps they need to go through in order to complete the enquiry.

For Activity 2, you could provide pupils with a copy of diagram D. Allow them to highlight the relevant points in different colours to save them having to write out the information.

Provide a writing frame for the report including the headings shown below.

- The need for fair trade
- What a fair trade company needs to do
- What the coffee growers will give in return
- The effects of fair trade on people living in the UK
- The effects of introducing fair trade

### For higher-ability pupils

Ask these pupils to find out more information about fair trade by using the Fairtrade website (www.fairtrade.org.uk). They could find out:

- who needs fair trade
- the range of fair trade products available
- an example of a fair trade producer and the impact that fair trade has had on the producer. You could suggest the decline of banana farmers in the Windward Islands.

Ask pupils to include this information as part of their report.

# 6 Key skills: maps and diagrams

**Pupil Book pages 106–107**

# How can we use an atlas?

## About this spread

In this spread pupils are introduced to the use of an atlas and the kind of information that they provide. The aim is to show pupils a number of different types of map, including ones that show human and physical information. It also shows pupils political maps that show detail such as the borders between countries and capital cities, physical maps that show relief, and others such as choropleth and thematic maps that show specific information such as population, land use and employment.

## Learning outcomes

By the end of this spread pupils should be able to:

- divide maps into categories
- use a political map
- use a choropleth map

## Key vocabulary

- physical map
- political map

## Learning objectives

On this spread pupils should learn:

- to identify and categorise different types of map
- to know how and where to find information in an atlas.

## Skills builder

Being familiar with an atlas and the types of maps that you will find in them is an important skill for the pupils to learn. Pupils can practise using the contents to find maps of countries and the index to find specific places. There also needs to be an awareness of the other maps that they might find in an atlas and the way that they display information such as choropleth maps of vegetation or rainfall.

## Further discussion suggestions

- Which type of data is linked to which type of map?
- What do star and planet maps show?

## Answers to activities

1 a **Physical**
   British Isles: July temperature
   Europe: Relief
   Asia: January temperatures
   World: Natural disasters
   Africa: Pressure and winds

   **Political**
   Africa: Countries
   World: Political

   **Other**
   British Isles: Farming
   Europe: Living standards
   Asia: Population trends
   North America: Land use
   World: Rich and poor

b **Other physical maps**
   World: Major rivers
   Indian Ocean: Depth contour (bathymetric) map
   Antarctica: Height of glaciers

   **Other political maps**
   South Africa: Provincial boundary map
   Germany: Major towns and cities
   UK: Administrative boundaries map

   **Other maps**
   World: Gross Domestic Product
   South East Asia: Literacy Rate
   UK: London Underground map

2 a 12 (Note that Guiana is not a country but a French overseas department.)

  b Argentina, Buenos Aires
    Bolivia, La Paz
    Brazil, Brasilia
    Chile, Santiago
    Colombia, Bogotá
    Ecuador, Quito
    Guyana, Georgetown
    Paraguay, Asunción
    Peru, Lima
    Uruguay, Montevideo
    Surinam, Paramaribo
    Venezuela, Caracas
    (Guiana, Cayenne)

3 a

| Town | Country | Natural vegetation | Annual Rainfall |
|---|---|---|---|
| Buenos Aires | Argentina | Grassland and savanna | 500–1000 mm |
| Lima | Peru | Desert | Under 250 mm |
| La Paz | Bolivia | Alpine and high plateau | 500–1000 mm |
| Manaus | Brazil | Tropical rainforest | 1000–2000 mm |
| São Paulo | Brazil | Tropical rainforest | 2000–3000 mm |

  b Pupils' answers will vary depending on their choice of town.

# 6 Key skills: maps and diagrams

**Pupil Book pages 108–109**

## How can we describe physical features on a map?

### About this spread

This spread shows an upland area in the Lake District. The map features a number of steep-sided valleys with flat bottoms surrounding Ullswater. There are a number of other physical features that the pupils can observe such as woodlands and streams. Pupils are asked to look at the map in detail and interpret both the overall landscape that they can see, and also individual elements that, when added together, help to make sense of the bigger picture.

### Learning objectives

On this spread pupils should learn:

- to use contour lines to determine relief on a map
- to use map symbols to identify the key features
- to interpret a landscape by looking at a map.

### Learning outcomes

By the end of this spread pupils should be able to:

- identify how different types of slope are shown on the map
- be able to state what a landscape looks like by looking at the map
- to be familiar with different types of map symbol.

### Skills builder

Being able to interpret what a landscape looks like from a map is a difficult skill for pupils to master. By looking at the contour lines and working out where the high and low points are gives you an overall impression of the landscape. How close together the contour lines are shows how steep the slopes are and makes the interpretation of the landscape more complete. Looking at symbols such as spot heights or triangulation points can then help to finish visualising the map.

### Key vocabulary

- **physical geography**
- **relief**
- **contour**
- **spot height**
- **vegetation**

### Further discussion suggestions

- What contour patterns would a pupil expect to find in other areas of the country?
- How would features such as hanging valleys or truncated spurs be shown on a map?

### Answers to activities

**1**
1. Gentle slope C
2. Steep slope G
3. Narrow ridge D
4. Rocky outcrops H
5. Flat valley floor A
6. Steep-sided valley E
7. Round Hill F
8. Smooth shoreline B

**2** The area is part of the Lake District and is rugged and mountainous. The land is generally **steeply** sloping and is a mixture of rounded **hills** and narrow **ridges**. The highest peak, High Dodd, is over **500** metres in height. Most of the valleys in the area are **straight** and steep-sided. The southern part of the area is drained by three **streams** which flow into Ullswater. Most of the area is rough **moorland** with a few small areas of **woodland**. The north shoreline of Ullswater is mainly **smooth**. The south is more **uneven** and has some **bays**.

## 6 Key skills: maps and diagrams

**Pupil Book pages 110–111**

# How can we describe human features on a map?

### About this spread

Pages 108–109 dealt with the physical features that are found on a map. This spread looks at human features. The map shows the town of Dartmouth in Devon and the human activities that occur at this location. The River Dart flows through the middle of the map and it is the focus of many of the human activities that are found in this location, such as ferries, marinas and quays.

### Learning objectives

On this spread pupils should learn:

- to know the difference between physical and human features
- to use map symbols to identify the key features
- to interpret a landscape by looking at a map.

### Learning outcomes

By the end of this spread pupils should be able to:

- identify how human activity is shown on a map
- find individual features on the map using symbols
- interpret a landscape by looking at a map.

### Key vocabulary

- physical features
- human features

### Skills builder

Being able to read Ordnance Survey maps and look at the way that they display information is a key skill for pupils to know. By looking at the map symbols, pupils can build up an image of what the area is like and then they can interpret what human activities can occur in this location.

### Further discussion suggestions

- Would Dartmouth be a good place for you to go on holiday?
- What tourist activities could you set up in Dartmouth and where would you locate them?

### Answers to activities

**1**
1. Farm C
2. Main road E
3. Minor road H
4. Ferry D
5. Woodland A
6. River Dart B
7. Tourist facility F
8. Coastal walk I
9. Water activities G

**2** Each answer is used once in this order, This part of south Devon has few **villages** but many small farms scattered across the area. The largest town is **Dartmouth**. It is on the **west** bank of the River Dart.

Communications are poor with only one **main road** serving the area. A few **minor roads** give access to other parts of the area. A number of **ferries** cross the River Dart. The area is mainly **rural** with most of the land given to farming. **Tourism** is also important, with several **car parks**, walks and **camp sites** available.

## 6 Key skills: maps and diagrams

**Pupil Book pages 112–113**

# What do choropleth maps show?

### About this spread

This spread is designed to give pupils practice at reading and drawing choropleth maps showing that they can understand how the data is represented using gradual shading. The pupils also have an opportunity to complete their own choropleth maps so that they can see how important it is to choose the correct categories and colours to ensure that there is a clear pattern. Pupils also have the opportunity to practise the skill of describing the pattern that they have identified on the map.

### Learning outcomes

By the end of this spread pupils should be able to:

- read a choropleth map accurately
- identify and describe what a choropleth map shows
- draw their own choropleth map.

### Key vocabulary

- choropleth map

### Learning objectives

On this spread pupils should learn:

- to use gradual shading to understand how to read choropleth maps
- to describe what a map shows.

### Skills builder

Describing a pattern on a map should follow three stages. The first stage is to identify where the highest values on the map are and what value they represent. The second stage is to identify where the lowest values are on the map and what value they represent. Finally, pick out a value from the middle and use data to comment on it. This will depend on how many categories there are between the highest and lowest value. If there is a particular anomaly this may also be worth describing. There is no need to provide a reason as it does not ask for an explanation.

### Further discussion suggestions

- How do you decide what groups to divide the data into?
- What are the best colours to use to highlight the patterns clearly?

### Answers to activities

1. **a** Fort William
   Keswick
   Aberystwyth
   Penzance

   **b** Britain's wettest area is the north **west**.
   Britain's driest area is the south **east**.
   Rainfall decreases from **west** to **east**.

2. The biggest average weekly spend is in the South East and East Anglia with an average of over £550. The lowest is in Northern Ireland with an average weekly spend of £469. As you move north and west in England the average weekly spend decreases from a high of £614 in the South East to between £480 in the North.

3. Ensure pupils have a key and a title for their map. Pupils should work out what colour each region is going to be before they start. The categories should be balanced to give a meaningful map.

# 6 Key skills: maps and diagrams

**Pupil Book pages 114–115**

## How can we use diagrams in geography?

### About this spread

Diagrams are a key method of imparting information to the reader as they can highlight key ideas, patterns or the flow of information much more clearly than a solid block of text. In this spread pupils break down the process of creating a diagram into constituent parts so that they get a clear understanding. They also look at a range of different diagrams and have the chance to select the most appropriate one for the information that they wish to represent.

### Learning objectives

On this spread pupils should learn:
- the types of diagram they can use
- to identify the steps involved in creating a diagram.

### Learning outcomes

By the end of this spread pupils should be able to:
- know what advantages there are of using a diagram
- decide which diagram to use
- select appropriate information to create a diagram.

### Skills builder

The construction of diagrams is a key skill for pupils to master. It can convey a complex idea quickly allowing them to access information more easily. The first skill for the pupil to master is selecting what information to show from all that is available. This could include key words, data or explanations. When this has been done, the next step is to decide which type of diagram would be the best to represent the information. The final skill that this spread tries to build is to provide an opportunity for pupils to break down all of the relevant information in to small chunks and fit it together logically making sure that all of the relevant information is used.

### Further discussion suggestions

- What other kinds of diagrams could the pupil use?
- How can you convert a spider diagram into a mind map?
- How can you use colour to make a diagram more complex?

### Answers to activities

**1** Spider diagram with "How can we use diagrams in Geography?" at the centre, surrounded by:
- A diagram breaks complex ideas into smaller components
- You can see the sequence of different ideas
- It is easy to highlight the key points in a diagram
- The viewer can take in more information quickly
- A diagram presents the information visually

**2** What happens when a volcano erupts

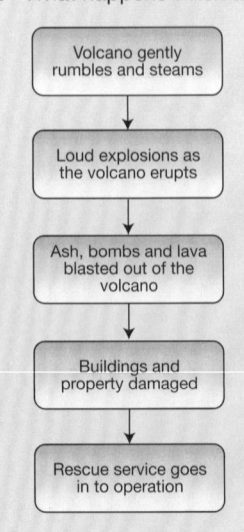

Flowchart:
- Volcano gently rumbles and steams
- Loud explosions as the volcano erupts
- Ash, bombs and lava blasted out of the volcano
- Buildings and property damaged
- Rescue service goes in to operation

Trade in more developed countries

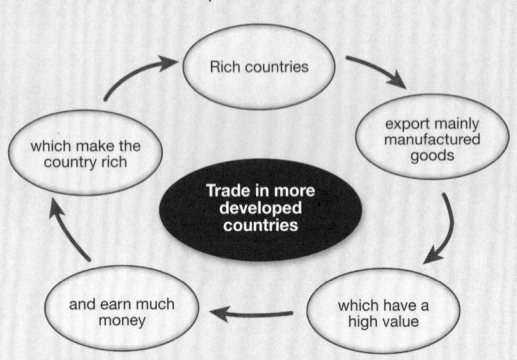

Cycle diagram: Rich countries → export mainly manufactured goods → which have a high value → and earn much money → which make the country rich → Rich countries

Location factors for a car assembly works

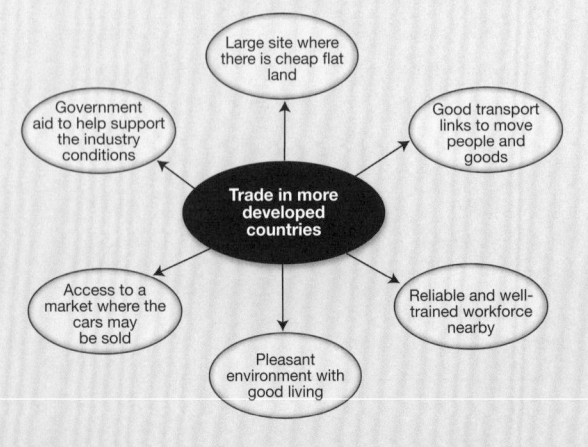

Spider diagram with "Trade in more developed countries" at the centre, surrounded by:
- Large site where there is cheap flat land
- Good transport links to move people and goods
- Reliable and well-trained workforce nearby
- Pleasant environment with good living
- Access to a market where the cars may be sold
- Government aid to help support the industry conditions

**3** Students would be expected to complete a flowchart with the more able students adding more steps. Boxes could contain details of type of vehicle, length of journey, number of passengers or the route taken on the journey.

# 6 Key skills: maps and diagrams

**Pupil Book pages 116–117**

## What are population pyramids?

### About this spread

Population pyramids are diagrams that can be used to display the population of a specific country or region. Breaking down the information into age categories and displaying the percentage of males and females allows for an analysis of the data from which conclusions can be drawn. This spread allows pupils to look at the different patterns that a population pyramid can show and links them to the type of country that they represent. Pupils are given the opportunity to practise drawing a population pyramid and avoid some of the errors that can occur in the process.

### Learning outcomes

By the end of this spread pupils should be able to:

- know what a population pyramid shows
- interpret what different population pyramids show
- construct a population pyramid.

### Key vocabulary

- age–sex pyramids
- developed country
- developing country

### Learning objectives

On this spread pupils should learn:

- to compare the percentage of people in different age groups
- to help forecast future population growth
- how to draw a population pyramid.

### Skills builder

This spread provides pupils with the opportunity to interpret a graph. By looking at the statements provided they will see the distinctive shape of the graph and use it to select the correct sentence. When all of the sentences are collected together, this helps pupils to form an impression of what the country is like and whether it can be classified as a developed or developing country. Pupils are also given a chance to practise drawing a population pyramid.

### Further discussion suggestions

- Are there any further shapes that a population pyramid can exhibit?
- Predict what problems an ageing society can suffer from.
- What reasons cause changes in the shape of population pyramids?

### Answers to activities

**1 a** Population pyramids show:
  - the percentage or the number of people in different age groups
  - the balance between male and females.

  **b** Population pyramids enable comparisons to be made between countries and to help in forecasting future trends in population. This allows any potential problems to be identified and for plans to deal with these problems to be put in place in good time.

**2** Correct statements are:
  - The graph is triangular in shape.
  - There are decreasing numbers in each age group.
  - 25 per cent of the population is less than 10 years old.
  - There is a small proportion of older people.
  - There is a high proportion of young people.
  - There are few elderly people.
  - Male and female numbers are similar.

**3 a** Students should complete the graph adding percentages for categories 20–29 to category 80+.

  **b** Statements that are accurate for the graph include:
  - The graph is tall and narrow.
  - There are almost equal numbers in each age group.
  - There is a low proportion of young people.
  - Male and female numbers are similar.

  **c** UK population growth will be slow as there are few children being born (around 6% of the population is under 9 years old) and people are living longer (8.7% of males and 11.8% of females are more than 60 years old).

# Appendix 1 — The economic activity enquiry checklist

## Section 1 — The Introduction

*Have you:*                                                                                    Student    Assessor

- included a title                                                                              ☐          ☐
- copied table A and completed it by adding what attractions your ideal coastal resort should have?  ☐   ☐

## Section 2 — Map reading skills and photo interpretation

*To succeed make sure you:*                                                                    Student    Assessor

- can state directions, measure distances by use of the scale, recognise heights from contour lines and spot heights, and quote 4 figure and 6 figure grid references from a 1:50000 Ordnance Survey map   ☐   ☐
- can orientate an Ordnance Survey map and an aerial photograph                                 ☐          ☐
- use the Ordnance Survey map B to answer the questions in table C correctly.                   ☐          ☐

## Section 2 — The main part: is Porthcawl the right place?

Make sure you have you learnt enough about Porthcawl from map B and photo D to allow you to decide whether or not you would want to spend a holiday in the resort by:     Student    Assessor

**a**
- listing the types of accommodation provided in the resort                                     ☐          ☐
- listing examples of your three ideal physical attractions listed in table A found in Porthcawl   ☐       ☐
- listing examples of your three ideal human attractions listed in table A found in Porthcawl     ☐       ☐
- listing other physical attractions of Porthcawl that would attract you to the resort           ☐          ☐
- listing other human attractions of Porthcawl that would attract you to the resort              ☐          ☐

**b**
- Using a correct four- or six-figure grid reference, whichever is appropriate, to give examples where your family can enjoy their interest in walking, wildlife, sport, beach games and history.   ☐   ☐

## Section 3 — Conclusion

*Decide whether or not your family would like to visit Porthcawl by:*                          Student    Assessor

**a**
- drawing a sketch map of the area showing the coastline and the approximate area covered by Porthcawl    ☐   ☐
- giving your sketch map a title, a north point, a scale and a key                              ☐          ☐
- adding labels to your map to show the physical and the human attractions of the area for tourists   ☐   ☐
- making sure the heads of the arrows are correctly positioned on the attraction labelled       ☐          ☐
- classifying the attractions into *human* and *physical* by colour coding them **green** or **red**   ☐   ☐
- adding the meaning of the two colours to the key                                              ☐          ☐

**b**
- writing a summary, giving reasons for your decision as to whether or not your family would want or visit Porthcawl.   ☐   ☐

**Extension**

*To really develop your answer:*

- describe some other factors not evident on the map or the photo that may influence your decision as to whether or not your family would want to spend a holiday in Porthcawl   ☐   ☐
- explain how the age and gender of the different members of your family may give them differing opinions as to whether or not they wish to go on holiday to Porthcawl.   ☐   ☐

# Appendix 2 — The population enquiry checklist

## Section 1 — Data analysis and prediction

*Have you:*  **Student**

- made a large copy of table B on page 66 ☐
- analysed the information on each of the ten areas from drawing D on page 67 ☐
- listed the positive factors which might attract people to live in areas 1–10 ☐
- listed the negative factors which might attract people to live in areas 1–10 ☐
- evaluated the information you have gathered for each site ☐
    - decided if each area is 'crowded', 'in between' or has 'few' people ☐
    - given at least two reasons for each decision? ☐

## Section 2 — Data presentation and decision making

*Have you:*  **Student**   **Assessor**

- made a copy of map C on page 66 ☐ ☐
- colour-coded the map to show population density ☐ ☐
- included a key on your map ☐ ☐
- decided which areas are most likely to have a main town ☐ ☐
- located the three towns on your map ☐ ☐
- Named the:
    - towns ☐ ☐
    - mountain range ☐ ☐
    - rivers ☐ ☐
    - seas ☐ ☐
    - imaginary continent ☐ ☐
- coloured the coastline in blue? ☐ ☐

# Appendix 3: The India enquiry checklist

## Section 1 — The Introduction

*Have you:*                                                                 Student   Assessor

- described what the term 'development' means                                 ☐         ☐
- used the term 'standard of living'                                          ☐         ☐
- used examples to explain your answer                                        ☐         ☐
- described India's history of development using three headings              ☐         ☐
- used facts and figures that highlight these differences:                    ☐         ☐
    - up to 1900                                                              ☐         ☐
    - 1900 to 1950                                                            ☐         ☐
    - after 1950?                                                             ☐         ☐

## Section 2 — Main part

*To succeed make sure you:*                                                  Student   Assessor

- give each of the nine drawings in diagram C a heading                       ☐         ☐
- arrange the headings in a diamond shape as shown in diagram B               ☐         ☐
- draw three bar graphs to show information on drawings 10, 11 and 12         ☐         ☐
- arrange the bars as follows:
    - Wealth, highest income on the left                                      ☐         ☐
    - Education, most able to read and write on the left                      ☐         ☐
    - Food, highest-quality food supply on the left                           ☐         ☐

*Have you:*

- used a ruler                                                                ☐         ☐
- labelled the axes                                                           ☐         ☐
- added a title to each graph?                                                ☐         ☐

## Section 3 — Conclusion

*In your conclusion include:*                                                Student   Assessor

- evidence to show that India is a newly industrialized country with not quite the full signs of a developed country        ☐         ☐
- a description of how developed India is in social terms (include words such as *education, university, environment, health care, overwork*)        ☐         ☐
- a description of how developed India is in cultural terms (include words such as *traditions, cities, loyal, dress, family time, sports*)        ☐         ☐
- your agreement/disagreement with the fact that 'the Indians have a fast-growing economy that is helping to improve its standard of living'        ☐         ☐
- reasons why you agree/disagree.                                             ☐         ☐

### Extension

*To really develop your answer:*

- check that your conclusion includes a mix of economic, social and cultural factors.        ☐         ☐

# Appendix 4: The resources enquiry checklist

## Section 1 — Finding the facts

Before you finish your enquiry use the reminders below to make sure that you have covered all of the correct points.

**Did you find out:** — Student / Peer

- how much money goes to coffee growers ☐ ☐
- how much money ends up in Kenya ☐ ☐
- how much money ends up in the UK ☐ ☐
- where most of the extra money goes if the price of coffee in the shops goes up? ☐ ☐

**Thinking about the issues**

*What do you think may help:* — Student / Peer

- reduce poverty ☐ ☐
- improve conditions for growers ☐ ☐
- protect the environment ☐ ☐
- affect people in the UK? ☐ ☐

**Your report to Kenya Coffee** — Student / Peer / Assessor

- Comment on why there is a need for more fair trade companies. ☐ ☐ ☐
- Summarise what a fair trade company needs to do. ☐ ☐ ☐
- How would Kenya Coffee have to change? ☐ ☐ ☐
- Explain what coffee growers will give in return for the fair trade agreement. ☐ ☐ ☐
- How might they alter their farming practices and how they use the environment? ☐ ☐ ☐
- Explain the effect of Kenya Coffee becoming a fair trade company on people living in the UK. ☐ ☐ ☐
- How might this make trade fairer? ☐ ☐ ☐
- Conclude what would be the overall effects of making Kenya Coffee a fair trade company. ☐ ☐ ☐

# Notes

# Notes

# Notes